HISTORY OF THE GBEWAA KINGDOMS

New Edition

FUSHEINI YAKUBU

WORKBOOK PRESS LLC
187 E Warm Springs Rd,
Suite B285, Las Vegas, NV 89119, USA

Website: https://workbookpress.com/
Hotline: 1-888-818-4856
Email: admin@workbookpress.com

Ordering Information:
Quantity sales. Special discounts are available on quantity purchases by corporations, associations, and others.
For details, contact the publisher at the address above.

Library of Congress Control Number:
ISBN-13:   978-1-957618-96-8 (Paperback Version)
              978-1-957618-97-5 (Digital Version)

REV. DATE: 07/03/2022

HISTORY OF THE GBEWAA KINGDOMS

NEW EDITION

FUSHEINI YAKUBU

TABLE OF CONTENTS

ACKNOWLEDGEMENT

"Better late than never". This is a wise saying that reveals the reason for writing this book. Some people may be endowed with some special talents, which may be hidden. When such people are touched by some events to use the talents, the impact almost becomes beneficial to others. It is in this light I found myself.

Though I am related to the legend's family of Bimbilla, the talent would have been lost if I was not moved to act by some people. To be precise, I met my grandfather, Alhaji Abdulai who is the Chief Legend of Bimbilla (Lung-Naa). He showered on me oral tradition that has been passed on from our Great Great Grandfathers, from the reign of Naa Gbewaa to the current Kingdom of the three main Gbewaa Kingdoms (Dagbon, Mamprugu and Nanung).

The current chieftaincy crisis has chopped into the moral fiber of the society, causing us to lose or distort the oral tradition. I thought it prudent to document this enviable oral tradition in a form of a book that could be used as a reference point for the new generation. As a leader of an organization that cares for the youth, I am much particular about socio-cultural issues that will affect the youth and generations yet to come.

The General Public especially those who cannot understand Dagbani or read expressed their concerns. The request has been "why don't you write your oral tradition in English for us too to enjoy?" Hence the writing of this book: "HISTORY OF THE GBEWAA KINGDOMS".

There is a saying in Dagbani: "A Tree on top of a hill does not cry for height but size". Although I am related to the legend's family of Bimbilla who hold oral tradition, I needed to grow, and the growth was from other sources. I am therefore indebted to the sources, which helped me to grow to my present height.

My initial source was oral tradition where I had to go from one person to another gathering data/information. Those who helped me in this were the following people: Alhaji Abdulai (Chief Legend of Bimbilla), Bagli Naa Mahama Wumbei Mahami, Namburugu Community Elders, Mohammed Awal Mahama (Iron body), Mr. Inusah K. Dasoli, Vonaa Attah Abarika, Warikpamo Yahaya, Alhaji Braimah Damba (Bimbilla Tolon-Naa), Mr. Tia Robert Yakubu of Nalerigu Senior High School, Nayiri Bohagu II and his Elders and my elder brother, Alhaji Muhib Husein Kharma for the nice trip he arranged for me to visit Namburugu, not forgetting Nyong Lung-Naa Iddi Saaka.

Other sources from which I gathered my information were:

H. B. Martison, The Hidden History of Konkomba Wars in Northern Ghana.
D. S$_T$J. –P, Legends of Northern Ghana.
Hizkias Assefa, Coexistence and Reconciliation in the Northern Region of Ghana.
Peter Skalnik, Chiefdom at War with Chiefless People while the Kingdom Looks on.
Osei Kwadwo - An Outline of Asante History, Part 1- Third Edition.
Ibrahim Mahama - History and Tradition of Dagbon.
Cliff S. Maasole - The Konkomba and Their Neighbours.
Sekene-mody Cissoko - Histoire de l'afrique Occidentale.
Joseph Ki-Zerbo - Histoire de l'afrique Noire.
Intercontinental Shea Nuts Project.
Costheta Consults Gh. Ltd.
Millennium Youth Skills and Development Centre (MILLYSDEC).

I am very grateful to Mr. Adam Marshal (Forma Principal of Bimbilla E.P. Training College of Education and Historian) for editing this book. His contribution during the editing process has helped me to put the book into the desire sharp and content.

I am grateful to the Cultural Initiative Support Programme (CISP) with the small financial aid during data collection and training of a youth group in cultural drumming and dancing in the year 2007.

My sincere thanks go to Hannah Tratchman of IPA, Tamale office for her enormous support during the transfer of funds to 52 Novels in the US for the ebook conversion project.

Many people have contributed to the production of the book whose names did not appear. To them I say Thank you.

Finally, I thank God (Almighty Allah) for the good health, time, and other resources he has granted me to produce this book.

Thank you.

Fusheini Yakubu

INTRODUCTION

This book is a compilation of both oral tradition and information from early writers of history of the Gbewaa Kingdom and the great ancient Dagbon (Dabgon, Mamprugu & Nanung). It introduces readers to the oral tradition.

The main aim of the writer is to translate the oral tradition from the local language "Dagbani" into English for the public to appreciate the rich oral tradition of great Dagbon. The current chieftaincy crisis in the other two Kingdoms (Modern Dagbon & Nanung) makes the oral tradition to be prone to distortions by the society to suit their selfish interest at the expense of the new generation.

The information contained in the book was gathered from oral tradition sources and books mentioned in the acknowledgement. The writer was cautioned by the oral tradition sources not to add his own interest but the true oral tradition as it is forbidden by our great great grandfathers who have instituted it. Failure to do so will be a curse on the writer. The writer observed sacrifice from Bimbilla Lung-Naa (Chief Tomtom Beater) before the information was released to him due to the intricacy of the oral tradition of great Dagbon. The reason for referring to some books by initial writers was to trace the dates, as oral tradition could not provide.

The book also seeks to promote peaceful co-existence among ethnic groups and the chieftaincy divide that exist in Modern Dagbon and Nanung.

DEDICATION

I am dedicating this book to the great kings of the four main Gbewaa Kingdoms in Ghana and Burkina Faso, Mamprugu, Dagbon, Nanung and Mossi Kingdom. My dedication also goes to the following Gbewaa Chiefdoms: Builsa Chiefdom, Nabdan Chiefdom Talensi Chiefdom and Waala Chiefdom. My special dedication goes to Nayiri Naa Bohagu II (Mahami Abdulai), Yaa Naa Abubakari Mahama II, Late Bimbilla Naa Dassana Abdulai and the late Bimbilla Naa Abarika Attah II.

My dedication goes to the heroes in the Gbewaa Kingdoms as follows: H. E. Late Alhaj Aliu Mahama *(A Ghanaian Engineer, a Politician and Vice President of Ghana from 7th January 2001 to 7th January 2009. He was the Ghana's first Muslim Vice President)*, H. E. Dr. Mahamudu Bawumia *(A Ghanaian Economist, a Banker, and Vice President of Ghana)*, H. E. Dr. Mohammed Ibn Chambas *(A Nanumba, Ghanaian Lawyer, Diplomat, Politician and Academician who has served as an international civil servant since 2006. He last served as the United Nations Special Representative of the Secretary General for West Africa and the Sahel, and the Former Head of UNOWAS from April 2014 to April 2021)*, Honourable Lawyer Haruna Iddrisu *(A Ghanaian Lawyer, a Politician, MP for Tamale South Constituency and Minority Leader of Ghana's Seventh Parliament)*, Honourable Alhaj Inusah Fuseini Malizal Naa, Honourable A. B. Fusheini, Honourable Hajia Alima Mahama, Lawyer Ibrahim Mahama, Honourable Alhaj Iddrisu Mahama, Honourable Speaker of Parliament Alban Kingsford Sumana Bagbin, Honourable Mahama Ayariga, Late Honourable Hawa Yakubu, Pishigu-Lana Alhassan Andani *(A Ghanaian Economist and Chief Executive Director of Stanbic Bank Ghana Limited)*, Yogu-Lana Adam, Alhaji Abdulai Chairman, Alhaj Yahaya Iddi, Tolon Naa Yakubu Alhassan, Tolon Naa Major Abukari Sulemana, Gushegu Naa B. A. Bawa, Vo-Naa Imoro, Yoo Naa Yakubu Gnunbeikpang, Dr. David Abdulai (Dr. Gurugu), Gushegu Naa Abukari Alhassan Gbanzaba, Lawyer R. I. Alhassan *(First Lawyer in Dagbon)*, Joshua Amidu, Alhaj Chairman Sumani Zolikugli, Zaamigu Imam Sheik Adam *(A Ghanaian*

Islamic Preacher and Leader of Tamale Central Mosque), Late Sheik Zakaria Yussif Ajura *(A Ghanaian Islamic Preacher and Founder of Ambariya Sunni Community)*, Sheik Ibrahim Basha Iddrisu *(A Ghanaian Islamic Preacher, Founder of Nuriya Islamic Institute in 1969 and Leader of Masjidul Bayaan)*, Gulkpegu Naa Alhassan Mahama, Honourable Ramatu Baba *(First Female MCE, Yendi)*, Late Nyankpala-Lana J. S. P. Kalem, Alhaj Maandugu, Late Alhaj Abdulai Soja, Late Honourable Mustapha Ali, Late Dakpem Lung-Naa Alhaj Bababila, Late Abubakari Issah Moɣulo, Late Fusheini Jenjilin, Late Tolon Lung-Naa Adam Gbaw, Late Kpihibara Lung-Naa Dogbura, Nanton Naa Bawa Mahama, Late Nanton Naa Sulemana Alhassan, Late Zoosali-Lana Charles Tia Sulemana, Sharif Gali *(Legend)*, Sirina Issah *(First Female Musician in Dagbon)*, Rashid Abdul Mugeez *(A Ghanaian Singer and Songwriter, born in Bimbilla, he became known through the influential Afrobeats/Hiplife duo R2Bees, which he formed with his Cousin Faisal Hakeem in 2007)* Sharifa Gunu *(She was born a princess into a royal family of the Kingdom of Dagbon, She was at one time the dance champion for the Northern Region, First Runner up for the 1998 National Dance Championship, then known as The Embassy Pleasure)*, Nba Sanda *(pioneer in Dagbani Drama)*, Alhaj Hamed Adam *(pioneer in Dagbani Drama)*, Mr. Neindow (pioneer in Dagbani Drama), Lawyer Gbuɣanli *(pioneer in Dagbani Drama)*, Afa Tafirili *(pioneer in Dagbani Drama)*, Alhaj T. B. Damba *(Founder Amasachina & Former Ambassador to Saudi Arabia)*, Ten-bobli Abdulai, Prince Mahama, Ziblim Bandamda, Professor Haruna Yakubu *(First Dagomba Vice Chancellor, UDS)*, Sagnarigu Naa Dr. Ziblim Andani, Bripeil-Naa Paul, Duunying Naa Von Salifu, Professor Nabila, Adam Adu Marshal *(First graduate in Nanung)*, Dalun-Lana Abdulai Mahama *(Longest serving chief in Dagbon)*, Yalezoli-Lana Salifu Abdul-Rahaman, Yalezoli-Gaa Naa Hawa Abdulai *(A Banker and Queen Mother)*, Dakpam Naa Charles Natogmah Attah *(First MP for Dagbon Nanung Constituency & Deputy Defense Minister during Ghana First President Dr. Kwame Nkrumah regime)*, Alhaj Mohammed Abdulai Baba *(First Nanumba to become Northern Regional Minister during Ghana's President Dr. Hilla Limann)*, Honourable Salifu Sa-eed *(Longest serving Northern Regional Minister during Nana Addo Dankwa Akufu Addo first four years in Government from 2017 to 7th January 2021)*, Mion Lana Abdulai Mahamadu *(First Dagbon Chief to serve Government*

Agency Governing Board, Board Member of NEDCo) Yoo Naa Yakubu Abdulai *(First Dagbon Chief to serve Government Agency Governing Board, Board Member of GNPC)*, Chamba Sung-Lana Alhaj Abdulai Alhassan Chambas *(First District Commissioner to Nanung, He later became the Municipal Commissioner of Tamale and facilitated the resettlement of Aboabu and Zogbeli in Tamale)* ,Alhaj Amidu Damba *(First Dagbani Radio Presenter at GBC)*, Sandema Nab Dr. Ayieta Azantilow *(Longest Served Chief in West Africa from 1931 to 14th November 2006, 75 years)* Paul Afoko *(A Politician and First Builsa to become National Chairman of NPP)*, Yani Gushie Naa Professor Abubakari Alhassan *(The Founder of Ghana Developing Communities Association, GDCA)*, Kuglana Mohammed Awal *(Dagbon Custom & Tradition Discussant on radio)* and among others.

I pray that Almighty Allah will continue to bless me with long life, good health, time, and the resources needed to publish a comprehensive book on **"The Heroes of Great Gbewaa Kingdoms"**. This book when published, will inspire the youth and generations yet to come, to also work hard. So, that one day their names and efforts will also be printed in gold to inspire the new generations. Our revered heroes acknowledged above should expect me to visit them in the near future for comprehensive information on their contributions to the growth and development of Gbewaa Kingdoms and Ghana at large.

CHAPTER ONE

THE ORIGINS OF DAGBAMBA

1.0 Pathogenesis of the Aboriginal Dagbamba

Both written and oral literature had it that the ordinary Dagomba man arrived in ancient Dagbon before the rulers (Naa Gbewaa and his descendants). According to Tamakloe, when Naa Nyagsi and his father "Naa Sitobu" arrived in modern Dagbon about the year 1416, the ordinary man was already in Dagbon. Tindaanba (Fetish Priest or Landowners) headed communities. According to Rattray, with the advent of the rulers of Great Dagbon, the common Dagomba like other tribes of Northern Ghana were already occupying the areas they are today.

By oral literature, the ordinary "Dagbamba" of Mamprugu, Dagbon and Nanung were already occupying the territories they occupy today when Naa Gbewaa arrived at Pusiga in the Upper East Region of Ghana. The inhabitants of Modern Dagbon, Mamprugu and Nanung were commonly known as Dagbamba at the time Naa Gbewaa arrived in Ghana. According to Ibrahim Mahama (a Tamale based lawyer and author of a book: History and Tradition of Dagbon), the name of these inhabitants of Mamprugu, Dagbon and Nanung is not just a historical fact, but also indeed a linguistic-cultural reality of our time. He further indicated that, the inhabitants of the three sister Kingdoms do not only speak the same language and possess similar cultures but they still sometimes, if not always, refer to themselves as Dagbamba.

Oral literature could not provide the period the ancestors of these aboriginal Dagbamba arrived in Ghana. The only method of record keeping they could explore by then was oral tradition, which has been passed on from generation to generation. As such vital information has been lost and very little has been written about the aboriginal Dagbamba.

The absence of archaeological evidence also makes it difficult to know the probable time the aboriginal Dagbamba arrived in Northern Ghana. The archaeological study conducted at Yani-Dabari (Old Yendi) by Shinnie, and Ozanne only aided to determine the time of arrival of the descendants of Naa Gbewaa in Northern Ghana. Yani-Dabari is the first settlement of the later immigrants; the descendants of Naa Gbewaa who became the rulers of Great Dagbon about the 13th century.

Based on the scanty evidence we have as regarding the time of the arrival in Ghana of the aboriginal Dagbamba, is to probably say that they arrived in Northern Ghana many years before the advent of the rulers of Great Dagbon.
Ancient or Great Dagbon comprises the lands of the Kings of Modern Dagbon, Mamprugu and Nanung.

Tamakloe, the earliest writer on Dagbon and Nanung considers the Dagbamba to be descendants of the Ad, a race that inhabited Arabia many years before the advent of Islam. "It is said that, after the confusion of tongues, the tribe of Ad; the son of Uz, the son of Aram, son of Shem, son of Noah settled in the Province Hadramout where their posterity greatly multiplied. This tribe continued to worship God but with time, they fell from the worship of true God into idolatry. God seeing this sent them the Prophet Heber to preach and reclaim them. But when they refused to acknowledge his mission, God sent a hot and suffocating wind, which blew for seven nights and eight days together and which entering into their nostrils passed through their bodies and destroyed them all and saved the very few who had believed in Heber. This tribe we learned were of prodigious stature, the tallest of them being said to be a hundred cubits or a hundred and fifty feet in heights and the least of them sixty cubits or ninety feet. This tribe, it is said wondered towards the

East and the West, settling in uninhabited countries, till they arrived in the country which is today called 'Dagbon' and their progeny were called Dagbamba[4]"

Tamakloe attributed the name of Dagbon to the skin on which the Ad Fetish Priests sat. Skin in Dagbani (language) is called gbon. He wrote: "The Chiefs or Fetish Priests among these settlers sat on cow skins and used various ornamented lion and tiger skins as their authority they called 'Ada gbon' meaning Ad's Skin. Hence, the name of the country now corrupted to Dagbon and the inhabitants 'Dagbamba[5]' so as far as Tamakloe is concerned the Dagbamba are descendants of Noah. When they arrived in Ghana, they settled at various places including Gunayili near Karaga and Yogo near Savelugu. After some years, some of them migrated to Nanumba and Adele in the Northern part of the Volta Region of Ghana. Further studies on the aboriginal Dagbamba conducted in recent times revealed that, the aboriginal Dagbamba first settled at Bagli community in the present day Karaga District. They came and met one man called Namogu whose clan was the legends before Namo-Naa Bizung, son of Naa Nyagsi. After he was integrated into the aboriginal Dagbamba society by marriage. The inter-marriages brought about different clans among the aboriginal Dagbambas as Gbandari, Nanmoglinsi, Langori and Kpariba. The aboriginal Dagbamba got their Tindaansili (Fetish Priest) from the Shengwan Tradition at the mountains of Kigali. They started spreading from Bagli to Namburugu and to other parts of great Dagbon such as Salaa, Gunayili, Yogo etc. after some years, some of them migrated to Nanumba and Adele in the Northern part of Volta Region of Ghana. It is based on this background that the Bagli Tindana is the head of Tindaanba in the three sister Kingdoms. Bagli Naa Mahama Wumbei Mahami with an interview confirmed that, Bagli community was the first settlement of their ancestors. After some years, some of them moved to settle at Namburugu and other parts of the three sister Kingdoms of Naa Gbewaa. According to him, the Bagli Skin Title is not only the head of Tindaanba but also the most senior title over Yaa Naa's title, Mamprugu Nayiri and Bimbilla Naa. As such they appellate Bagli Naa as "Namazaa Kpema, Namazaa Biya" meaning "Bagli Naa is the senior most as well as junior title over the titles of the three sister Kingdoms of Naa Gbewaa". The junior aspect of Bagli title is an expression that indicates the limited land, communities, and sub-titles under Bagli Naa's jurisdiction as compared to that of Yaa Naa, Mamprugu Nayiri and Bimbilla Naa. This means Bagli title is the senior most but has limited resources and power.

Figure 1: Fusheini Yakubu & Bagli Naa Mahama Wumbei Mahami

Figure 1: Diagrammatic Presentation of Tindaanba in Modern Dagbon.

Bagli Tindana/Naa

Namogu	Gbandari
Gushie Tindana	Langoyu Tindana
Namburugu Tindana	Kparigu Tindana
Salaa Tindana	Safam Tindana
Yong Dooni Tindana	Tamalgu Tindana
Yong Dakpem Tindana	Zaankal Tindana

Figure 2: Diagrammatic Presentation of Tindaanba in Nanung

Nabang Tindana (Juo)

Daalana	Sirikpamo Tindana
Kpandigli Ponaa	Kpandigli Ponadow
Varili Tindana (Jilo)	Lanjiri Tindana
Wumpiyu Tindana (Tagnamo)	Suburi Tindana
Varibeigu Tindana (Nakpa)	Kakuhi Tindana
Kumbo Tindana	Sunkuli Tindana (Wulensi)

These are some of the Tindaanba in Dagbon and Nanung.

Again, some of them also settled in the present day Mamprugu. Since Tamakloe was writing about modern Dagbon, he limited his scope to the inhabitants of modern Dagbon. The Tindaanba whom Tamakloe called Dagbamba inhabited not only modern Dagbon but also the sister Kingdoms of Mamprugu and Nanung. These three sister Kingdoms called themselves Dagbamba not because of their great ancestor 'Naa Gbewaa' but their predecessors "the Tindaanba of Ancient Dagbon who called themselves Dagbamba[1]". It must be emphasized that, it was the progeny of these Ads that Naa Tohogu of Mamprugu, Naa Sitobu or Nyagsi of Dagbon and Naa Gmantambu of Nanung met when they arrived in Great Dagbon.

Tamakloe has offered only little evidence for concluding that the Dagbamba are descendants of the Ad. He referred to the fact that modern day Dabgon was once inhabited by giants known as Tiawomia or Kondor. Certainly, the presence of giants in ancient Dagbon without more is no proof that the giants of the Ad are necessarily progenitors of the giants of ancient Dagbon.

1.1 Culture and Language

Critical examination of the culture and language of the Dagbamba, however, justified the view that the Dagbamba may in fact be descendants of the Ad of some other Arabian peoples. The language of the Dabgamba, which is Dagbani, has a multitude of words originating from Arabic. Some of the words are very fundamental, such that they may not be acquired in recent times when the Dagbamba had contact with Arabia at the advent of Islam. According to early writers, the history of Islam in Dagbon and the other two sister Kingdoms started in the mid 17th century by Hausa people. The table below shows some of the Dagbani words with Arabic roots.

1.2 Arabic Roots of Some Dagbani Words

	DAGBANI		ARABIC EQUIVALENT	
NO.	**WORD**	**MEANING**	**PRONUNCIATION**	**MEANING**
1	Saawara	Consultation	Mushaawara	Consultation
2	Albalaayi	Calamity	Al-balaay	Distress. misfortune
3	Alaafee	Health	Al-aafiya	Health. wellbeing
4	Halli	Temper	Haala	Make a great fuss;
5	Ashili	Secret	Al-siru	Secret
6	Asiba	Morning	Al-sabaah	Morning
7	Ala iziba	Surprise	Al-ajiiba	Surprise; strange; odd
8	Gari	To confuse	Garra	To surprise, dazzle someone
9	Zuli	Tail	Ziilum	A tail
10	Ninsala	Human being	Insaan	Human being
11	Zuliya	Offspring, descendants	Zuriya	Descendants
12	Niya	Intention	Niya	Intention
13	Aniya	Thought, to try	Niya	Intention
14	Yigunaadam	Human being	Ibn Adam	Son of Adam (Human Being)
15	Gaafara	Excuse, pardon	Gafara	To forgive
16	Yigsi	To get up, wake	Ishi	Wake up

1.3 Days of The Week

DAGBANI	MEANING	ARABIC	MEANING
Alahiri dali	Sunday	Yawimi Al-ahad	Sunday
Atani dali	Monday	Yawimi Alitan	Monday
Atalata dali	Tuesday	Yawimi Altalata	Tuesday
Alaba dali	Wednesday	Yawimi Al-Arba'a	Wednesday
Alamisi dali	Thursday	Yawimi Al-Khamis	Thursday
Alizima dali	Friday	Yawimi Al-Juma	Friday
Asibiri dali	Saturday	Yawimi Al-Sabt	Saturday

These were some of the words the Dagomba language came with since the ancient Dagbon. It is our view that the Dagomba through Islam did not acquire these words but by virtue of their origin from the Ad people, who belonged to pre-Islamic Southern Arabia extending from Umman at the mouth of the Persian or Arab Gulf to Hadhramault and Yemen at the southern end of the Red Sea. Today the words have significantly changed in their form and sound in the three sister Kingdoms of Great Dagbon, but their meaning remain the same.

Another convincing factor is the colour of the aboriginal Dagbamba, which gives credence to the view that they were of Arab complexion. Old school of oral tradition also indicated that the Tindaanba were all "red". Red is the word the Dagbambause when they mean fair or coloured in complexion.

Tamakloe again considers the fire festival of the Dagbamba as a custom emanated from Noah's time in commemoration of the day the Ark of Noah "rested on Mount Ararat and the people in the Ark came and made fires[7]". Dagbamba tradition attributes the significance of the fire festival to Prophet Noah; they assign different reasons for the festival. According to the tradition, when Prophet Noah was about to set out with his Ark one of his sons got missing. A search for him was commenced. The search continued until night when the son was not yet found. Searching lights were lit to look for him. The significance of the Fire Festival therefore is to commemorate the search for Prophet Noah's son. Whatever the reason, the tradition agrees that the Fire Festival relates to Prophet Noah and the Great Flood.

Furthermore, the lunar month for the Fire Festival (Bugum Goli) is the beginning of the year in the three sister Kingdoms: Dagbon, Mamprugu and Nanung. The same month is the beginning of the year in Arabia. New Year resolutions are made during the festival and also pray to God for protection, guidance, and prosperity. As part of the celebration, they cut bits and pieces of cooked food and put the same short on dividing walls in their houses. These pieces are supposed to be food for their ancestors and deceased family members. This pagan practice is certainly one of the practices that Tamakloe refers to as their fall "from the worship of true God into idolatry". Commenting on the Fire Festival, Blair wrote: "The big annual festival of Konkomba and other complete pagans' is their Fire Festival, the burning of the bush and fire rites in general. We can comfortably assume certainly that the Fire Festival existed in Dagomba prior to Muslim immigration[8]".

The Dagomba, like the Arabs, have twelve lunar months in a year. Even though the names of their months differ, their year begins with the same month. They also end the year with the same month. The number of days in their months is equal. A month is either thirty or twenty-nine days.

There is no direct oral or written evidence as to the period the Ad lived. But it is known that the cousins and successors of the Ad; the Thamud lived in 715 B.C. [9]

Some African writers claimed that "some tribes in Africa such as the Yuraba people have lived in their present area for thousands of years, and are not migrants from Arabia or Ethiopia," it may be so for some few African tribes and not generally all African tribes. The few evidence provided about the origins of the aboriginal Dagbamba justified their origins as descendants of Prophet Noah and for that matter the Ad.

1.4 The Aboriginal Dagbamba Clan System.

The aboriginal Dagbamba were made up of the following clans and professional groupings: Gbandari, Langori, Kpariba, Nanmonglinsi, Luɣipuna, Saɣiyelsi and Karenchaɣi. The Laabansi in the present-day Dagbon were descendants of Arab migrants from Morocco. The Aboriginal Dagbamba had some form of administrative and professional structures.

1.4.1 Gbandari: They were the military for the aboriginal Dagbamba. They were also, responsible for the construction of roads and footbridges. Today, the Gbandari can be traced to the worrier clans "Sapashinima" in Dagbon, Nanung and Mamprugu.

1.4.2 Kpariba: They are referred to us as "Dagbansabla". Most people call them Zabaɣa-kpariba. It is very wrong to call them Zabaɣa-kpariba because they are one of the Aboriginal Dagbamba clans in ancient Dagbon. The area they occupy in the Gbewaa kingdom is called Kparigu. The Kparigu land can be located on the middle belt from Mamprugu through Modern Dagbon to Nanung. It is important to put it on record that Gonjas do not have Kpariba. The Gonja clan mostly found in the East Gonja is called "Nterepu". It is marriage relationship that exist between the Kpariba and Gonjas and not descendants.

1.4.3 Nanmonglinsi: They were the legends of Ancient Dagbon before Naa Nyagsi killed the Namogu Tindana and enskinned his son, Namo-naa Bizung. The present-day Tomtom-beaters are descendants of Nanmonglinsi and Namo-Naa Bizung.

1.4.4 Luɣipuna: They were descendants of the Aboriginal Dagbamba and Slaves through marriage. It is very difficult to trace those who were Slaves and the Luɣipuna clan in Dagbon because they were integrated in the society.

1.4.5 Saɣiyelsi: They are Blacksmiths by profession and can be traced to Dagbon, Mamprugu and Nanung.

1.5 Pathogenesis of the Aboriginal Dagbamba and the Gbewaa Genotype.

Today, Dagombas, Mamprusi and Nanumbas in the three Gbewaa Kingdoms are descendants of the Aboriginal Dagbamba and Naa Gbewaa. Naa Gbewaa and his children arrived in Ancient Dagbon with the Gurima language which they abandoned and adopted the Dagbani language.

Cliff S. Maasole (the author of a book: The Konkomba and Their Neighbours) is of the view that, "Dagombas are of Zamfara origin, even though they often say that originally, they came from Gambaga. This source goes further to Kingdom that the Konkomba who are also of Zamfara origins settled before them[1]. This information suggests Konkomba anteriority vis-à-vis the Dagombas". This will rather lead us to a Kingdom of confusion and attempt to distort the history and oral tradition of Great Dagbon (Modern Dagbon, Mamprugu and Nanung). The rulers (descendants of Tohazie) of Great Dagbon could trace their roots to Zamfara and beyond. Tohazie was the only son of Tiyawumya. Tiyawumya came from King Shabarko family of Egypt. Tiyawumya was born in Massari. He moved to Thungi and from Thungi to Morroco. After some time, he later migrated to Chad and finally to Zamfara where he gave birth to Tohazie. Tohazie from Zamfara in Northern Nigeria moved to the Mali Empire. For detail information, refer to chapter 2 of this book.

According to Cliff S. Maasole that, the aboriginal Dagombas or Dagban Kpareba (black Dagbambas) as well as the giants known as Tiawomia or Kondor may probably be the Konkombas, is inadequate and has no proof. The probability that, the aboriginal Dagombas or Dagban Kpareba and the giants were Konkombas may lead us to the realm of speculation rather than of fact. *For more information on the aboriginal Dagbamba refer to the paragraphs above in this chapter.* The information provided by Cliff S. Maasole may be regarded as a shopping list of imaginative essays rather than a history or study in inter-ethnic relations in Northern Ghana. No wonder, Cliff S. Maasole that is the reason why you could not emboss your photograph on the book as the author, because you are not sure of the information.

18

Cliff S. Maasole further went on to indicate that, the Europeans and Germans were silent or do not acknowledge the sovereignty of Konkombas in Northern Territories is rather unfortunate and a blind argument. As such, it is baseless in the sense that their presence was insignificant in the Northern Territories. This is to say; only few of them were found in Eastern Dagbon "Zagbeli to be precise". In the case of Nanung, there was not even a single Konkomba in the Nanumba Traditional area during the time of the Germans from 1898 – 1917 (19 years). The Germans lasted for only 19 years in Nanung. One of the early Konkombas in Nanung settled at Kpatinga about 1942 with only a single cloth. He was thought how to farm Yam and they gave him Yam seeds free to start his own farm. This attracted a good number of Konkombas to come and settle in Nanung as they were aggressively looking for fertile lands to settle for farming. This was during the reign of Bimbilla Naa Abdulai. Even their migration to Nanung was because of the war they waged against Zagbeli-lana in modern Dagbon. Cliff S. Maasole failed to appreciate that, Konkombas are settlers in Great Dagbon (Modern Dagbon, Mamprugu and Nanung) and that was simply the reason why the German and European were silent over them.

The German colony was Northern Volta, Kpandai area, Bimbilla area, Yendi area, Zabzugu/Tatale area, Saboba/Cheriponi area up to Bawku (The Eastern Corridor) of the Republic of Ghana and present-day Republic of Togo. These areas were taken over by France and Britain as the League of Nations Trusteeship lands after the German left the place in 1917 because of First World War. West Gonja, West Dagbon, some parts of Nanung, Upper East, the Volta Region and Upper West fell under the British colony. After some time, a referendum was conducted by UN to decide whether the two Togos would stand apart or form a unitary Kingdom. It was based on the referendum that, Northern Volta, Kpandai area, Bimbilla area, Yendi area up to Bawku decided to join with Ghana for independence.

I would like to ask Cliff S. Maasole a very simple question as; the communities Konkombas occupied today in the Republic of Togo are their own lands or regarded as settlers? The answer certainly is that they are settlers in those communities because the indigenous people in those areas are Ewes, Kotokolis, Bassaris, Kabre and Bimobas.

However, this is not an att empt to mention all ethnic groups of the Republic of Togo but those who share boundaries with the Eastern Corridor of the Republic of Ghana. Most of these ethnic groups are in Ghana too.

CHAPTER TWO

2.0 EVOLUTION OF THE GBEWAA KINGDOMS

2.1 "Tohazie" The Red Hunter.

The history[11] of the Gbewaa Kingdoms, which is referred to us by some writers as the Rulers of Great Dagbon, begins with the story of a man popularly known as "Tohazie" Red Hunter. Tohazie was the only son of Tiyawumya. Tiyawumya came from King Shabarko family of ancient Egypt. Tiyawumya was born in Massari. He moved to Thungi and from Thungi to Morocco. After some time, he later migrated to Chad and finally to Gomba (Zamfara) where he gave birth to Tohazie. Tohazie from Zamfara in Northern Nigeria moved to the Mali Empire. By his profession as a hunter in Mali, he killed a wild cow that had prevented the people of the village from having access to water, and thereby saved them from dying of thirst. With time, he became very popular and even led the people in war to defeat their enemies in the region. The King of Mali rewarded Tohazie for his services and bravery. The reward included a princess of Mali who was given to him as a wife by the King of Mali. Tohazie's wife was a lame woman called "Pag-wobga". It was believed that there might be something special about her. For, Tohazie chose her in preference to other princesses who had been paraded by the King of Mali. The issue of the Malian Princess and Tohazie was Kpogunumbo the wonderful being. According to oral tradition, Tohazie and his wife did not live to see the manhood of their son Kpogunumbo. They both died when he was still a child. Kpogunumbo grew up and inherited his father. He showed bravery similar to that of his father in wars between the Malians and their neighbours. He moved westward of the Mali Empire and finally arrived at Biun in Gruma land. Kpogunumbo succeeded the Fetish King of Biun in a fight and took over his kingdom, which he ruled until his death.

Naa Gbewaa who is the grandson of Kpogunumbo ascended to the throne after the death of Kpogunumbo. After some years in Biun, Naa Gbewaa migrated with a large following to Pusiga in the Upper East Region of Ghana near the Ghana- Togo border. He continued fighting the wicked Tindaanba from Pusiga to Yani-Dabari by a way of expanding chieftainship to promote good governance and democracy. Even though the Tindaanba had some form of governance systems in their communities, but it was not centrally coordinated. For the wicked Tindaanba, rule was like survival of the fittest that Naa Gbewaa was fighting. The wicked ones were killed, and new chiefs replaced to rule the communities and the obedient ones made chiefs of their communities. Naa Gbewaa did not fight and drive indigenous people away; rather they were integrated into the society. Some writers perceive Dagombas, Nanumbas and Mamprusi as war like people but that may be a wrong conclusion. Because the aboriginal Dagbamba were living together in harmony before the advent of the descendants of Naa Gbewaa, who came with force and introduced chieftainship in the three sister Kingdoms of Great Dagbon. As such, Naa Gbewaa is regarded as the first King of Great Dagbon. Because Naa Gbewaa fought Tindaanba in a wide area, he was appellated as "Yogu -Tolana" meaning "warrior in a wide area". That is the reason why Yaa Naa, Nayiri of Mamprugu and Bimbilla Naa are also appellated as "Yogu -Tolana" because they are sons of Naa Gbewaa. Also, he was very powerful and the word "power" in Dagbani means "Yaa". The title Yaa Naa emanated from the powerful nature of Naa Gbewaa.

2.2 Naa Gbewaa Sons and Daughters.

Naa Gbewaa survived with a good number of children. According to some old school of oral tradition that Naa Gbewaa gave birth to nine children, others are of the view that the children were fifteen. Whatever it may be the most important thing is that, in his life, he gave birth to several children, but only seven (7) of them were very popular. First child was a female called Katchiogu (Pakpong

Katchiogu: Ofa Nam Cheri) or Yentaure; named by French. It is based on this, they praise every Princess (Pakpong) "Katchiogu", next was Zirli, Kufogu, Sitobu (Sigri-Nitobu, Duri-ni Nam), Tohagu (Galinkuna Tohagu) and Gmantambu. Other children of Gbewaa included Kuhu-Naa Shebeei, Sinson Naa Buhuyeligu, Karaga-Lana Beimoni (he was the last born of Naa Gbewaa), Zantandana Yirigipeili and Yemo-Karaga Lana Karateili. Oral tradition could not tell how long Naa Gbewaa ruled Great Dagbon; one can only say that he ruled Great Dagbon for several years.

Zirli and Kufogu, due to leadership and power struggled over the succession of the kingship, fought each other and Zirli defeated Kufogu. The reason was because the first child of Naa-Gbewaa was a female and by the tradition, a female does not inherit the father's property. These two brothers being next to the female daughter (Katchiogu) resulted in a succession dispute. After Zirli defeated Kufogu, he also died shortly. The tragic death of these two sons led to the death of Naa Gbewaa, he went out at Yani-Dabari and mysteriously entered the ground somewhere around Pusiga in the Upper East Region of Ghana. A round room was built round to signify the grave of the Great King and can still be located there today. This marked the burial of the three Great Kings (Yaa Naa, Bimbilla Naa and Nayiri) in the local round rooms at their various palaces. Some writers and old school of oral tradition had it that, Zirili succeeded Naa Gbewaa. This may lead us to a great confusion. Zirili died shortly after he killed Kufogu. Sitobu (Sigri-Nitobu) was then the elder son of Naa-Gbewaa and ascended to the throne after the death of Naa Gbewaa. Sitobu got married and gave birth to Nyagsi. Nyagsi grew up.

2.3 The Leadership of Naa Sitobu.

One day, Sitobu secretly told Nyagsi (his first son) to go and meet his uncles and tell them to seek for fortification in terms of war from their elder brother 'Naa Sitobu'. The two uncles (Tohagu and Gmantambu) went to their elder brother "Naa Sitobu" and proposed it to him but were refuted by him. Some days later, Naa Sitobu again asked Nyagsi to go back to remind his uncles. Naa Sitobu refused once again, the third reminder was sent again. Now, Naa Sitobu agreed to the proposal, but expressed his concern on how Nyagsi was going to fight without support. Tohagu agreed to go with him. Gmantambu then suggested that half of them with the ammunitions remain at home to guide the king (Naa Sitobu) and the two of them would use the other half of ammunitions to accompany Nyagsi to fight. The king finally agreed and brought out the ammunitions "Tobri". Everything being equal, they started the war towards Gambaga and when they got to Gambaga, they met a well to do woman who was the "Tindana" and for that matter the Queen of Gambaga with some few ethnic groups namely, Mamprusis, Tamplensi, Kussasi and Bimobas. According to the descriptions by oral tradition, the woman was short in height, fair in complexion with red hair "Zabgu", very rich in terms of animals such as Cattle, Sheep, Goat, Poultry, Horses, Donkeys as well as cash (Cowries were used as legal tender for the payment of goods and services). The Queen gave Nyagsi with his warriors' a warm reception. In every three (3) days' time Nyagsi will demand 100 each of the animals and cash to an extent that Nyagsi depleted the Queen's wealth. One day Nyagsi again demanded as usual, the Queen sent a reply to Nyagsi that, all the animals together would not reach 100. Nyagsi still insisted. The Queen remarked that, "I knew very well, he is here to kill me, and I am not going anywhere; he should come and kill me". On that faithful Friday, Nyagsi got prepared and beheaded the Queen. Oral tradition Kingdomd, "The Queen did not sheer blood but milk". Those who saw that said, they have killed a blessed child of God, by then there were some few Muslims (Hausas) and these people rubbed their bodies with the milk to also get the blessing. Nyagsi said they should give him some of the milk to also rub his body. When Nyagsi applied the milk on his forehead, he developed mental illness. Tohagu and Gmantambu in their effort to get treatment for Nyagsi could not work after they went round several communities seeking treatment from elders (Herbalist/Spiritualist). Finally, they decided to send Nyagsi back home to the king (Naa-Sitobu) for treatment. On their way back, they got to Savelugu, and an elderly (Herbalist/Spiritualist) offered them some treatment and the sickness subsided. According to oral literature, the Herbalist/Spiritualist gave them between three to seven days to be discharged and before he was discharged, Nyagsi's hair was shaved. The very day he was discharged emanated Savelugu chieftainship and the practice of shaving people's hair at funerals for chiefs and elders "Kuzabri". By then Naa-Sitobu had moved from Yani-Dabarini to Bagli and sent a message to them, to meet him at Bagli where he was staying with the Bagli Tindana. When they got to Bagli, they met Naa-Sitobu at the Bagli Tindana's palace. Naa-Sitobu mandated his son that same day to ascend to the throne secretly in the night and mysteriously entered the ground. It is for this reason that Sitobu cursed the sons of Naa Gbewaa not to visit Bagli forever. Surprisingly, Tohagu and Gmantambu came the following morning to greet their elder brother "Naa-Sitobu", only to see Nyagsi in the Chief's Insignia. A succession dispute arose again between Nyagsi and his uncles (Tohagu & Gmantambu). They got angry and were going back to prepare, to fight Nyagsi. Nyagsi sent some elders to call his uncles back and they were directed through the back door of the Tindana's palace where their elder brother was buried. Hence, this is where it begins; the practice of passing through the back door by elders and sub-chiefs to see the grave of any of the three main Kings of the three sister Kingdoms (Yaa-Naa, Bimbilla Naa & Nayiri) when any of them die.

2.4 Succession Dispute and the Partition of Gbewaa Kingdoms

Tohagu and Gmantambu got prepared to fight Nyagsi again after they realized, it was a planned thing, because by the tradition, they should have succeeded their elder brother (Naa-Sitobu) and groom Nyagsi but not Nyagsi to succeed his father (Naa-Sitobu). That was the reason why, they decided to fight and kill Nyagsi. Thank God, Bagli Tindana was a very good elderly person, who strongly intervened by directing them to proceed to Namburugu. When they got to Namburugu, they settled under a Baobab Tree. It was at this place the Bagli Tindana told them that it is at this place we are going to share your father's property to you. He told Naa Nyagsi that, your uncles knew their father's property and I in person knew about one of the properties that do not appear in a day light. It usually appears in the night and goes back in the night (the chief's insignia). For now, you have to produce all the properties that include Horses, Cattle, Sheep, Goat, Donkeys, Clothing, Money, Slaves and reserve the chief's insignia, tonight we will then finish the sharing. All the property was shared into three equal parts for the three of them. Tohagu, you are next to your brother Naa Sitobu, come and pick yours, followed by

Sitobu elder son 'Nyagsi', you represent your father Naa Sitobu, take your property and Gmantambu also take yours. Nyagsi you cannot seize our legacy and include us. We should have inherited our father's legacy including you but what your father did to you we cannot disskinned you. The skins were also shared equally into three. Hence, Yaa Naa, Nayiri and Bimbilla Naa are sitting on the same Gbewaa Skins. Tonight, the chief's insignia were equally shared into three for them. For that matter, the same insignia are used to enskin Yaa Naa, Nayiri and Bimbilla Naa. It is important to note that, the sharing of Gbewaa Skin and properties was facilitated by Bagli Tindana and assisted by Salaa Tindana, Namburugu Tindana and other Sub-Tindaanba in the Bagli area. As such Bagli Tindana is the head of Tindaanba in the three sister Gbewaa Kingdoms/kingdoms. Oral tradition Kingdoms that, "the nature of the Insignia makes the three main kings to always move in the night for confidentiality".

When they got their shares of the property and the Insignia, they became powerful and said this was what our father used to fight and capture lands we will also do same. This led to the separation of the three Sister Gbewaa Kingdoms into Modern Dagbon, Mamprugu and Nanung. Tohagu took the direction of Mamprugu and settled at Mamprugu. Gmantambu headed towards Yeji through Salaga to Attebubu. As at then Salaga and Yeji were not in existence. The only settlement was Attebubu with temporal structures such as thatch. After Naa Gmantambu, the Hausa people through the Trans-Shara Trade sought permission from the Bimbilla Naa and settled in Salaga. Interestingly, these Gonjas from Kpembe/Salaga were refugees from West Gonja and they came and sought refuge from Bimbilla Naa. Bimbilla Naa accepted them and gave them Chirifa old settlement "Chirifa Dabari" to settle. They were farming vegetables such as Okro, Keneaf, etc. for Nanumbas and the few Hausa people who were there. This gave birth to the Kpembe Skin. It is important to note that Kpembe Skin Title originated from Nanung Kingdom.

Before they separated from each other at Namburugu, they took an oath of succession and equity that; they are all equal in titles; under no circumstances shall Yaa Naa enskin Bimbilla Naa or Nayiri and vice versa. This accounts for the reasons why princes from Dagbon, Mamprugu and Nanung forbid visiting Bagli community.

Tong-Lana Yemusah, son of Naa Adan-Sigli, who attempted to break the record of "Bagli visit" mysteriously perished with his horse under a Baobab Tree that was closer to Bagli community. The Baobab Tree died in 2011. Moreover, this confirmed that, sons of Yaa Naa, Bimbilla Naa and Nayiri do not visit Bagli Community. Some writers and old school of oral tradition have it that, Mamprugu, Mossi and Modern Dagbon were founded between half of the 13th century to 14th century. What they failed to appreciate is the fact that, Naa Gbewaa ruled Great Dagbon (Modern Dagbon, Mamprugu and Nanung) for several years as one Kingdom or kingdom. After the death of Naa Gbewaa and Naa Sitobu resulted in a succession dispute among Nyagsi and his uncles (Tohagu & Gmantambu) that they separated at the same time at Namburugu and founded their individual Kingdoms/kingdoms and is today regarded as sister Kingdoms/kingdoms of Naa Gbewaa. Hence, as to whether the founding of Modern Dagbon and Mamprugu came after Nanung may lead us to the realm of speculation rather than of fact. Below are pictures of the two historic communities.

Bagli (A Historic Community of Great Dagbon)

Namburugu (A Historic Community of Great Dabon)

Namburugu Communtiy Showing the Spot Where the Gbewaa Skins/Titles "Nam" were Shared Among the three Great Sons of Naa Gbewaa (Nam Tariya Tuu-Gbuni).

The spot in the ancient times was sited with a very big Baobab Tree. The Tree died several years ago and currently with a grove of Nim Trees. The stones on which they sat and shared the property are available today under the grove. Nevertheless, Namburugu community still has many Baobab Trees today to justify the presence of Baobab Tree at the spot in the ancient times.

Mamprugu, Dagbon and Nanung are the three main sister Kingdoms/kingdoms of Naa Gbewaa in Northern Ghana. The other sister Kingdom/kingdom is the Mossi Kingdom in Burkina Faso. The Builsa Chiefdom, Nabdan Chiefdom, Talensi Chiefdom, and the Waala Chiefdom are the other smaller Kingdoms or chiefdoms of Naa Gbewaa in Northern Ghana. These Gbewaa Kingdoms are descendants of Naa Gbewaa and the Aboriginal Dagbamba who traced their origin to one ancestor's.

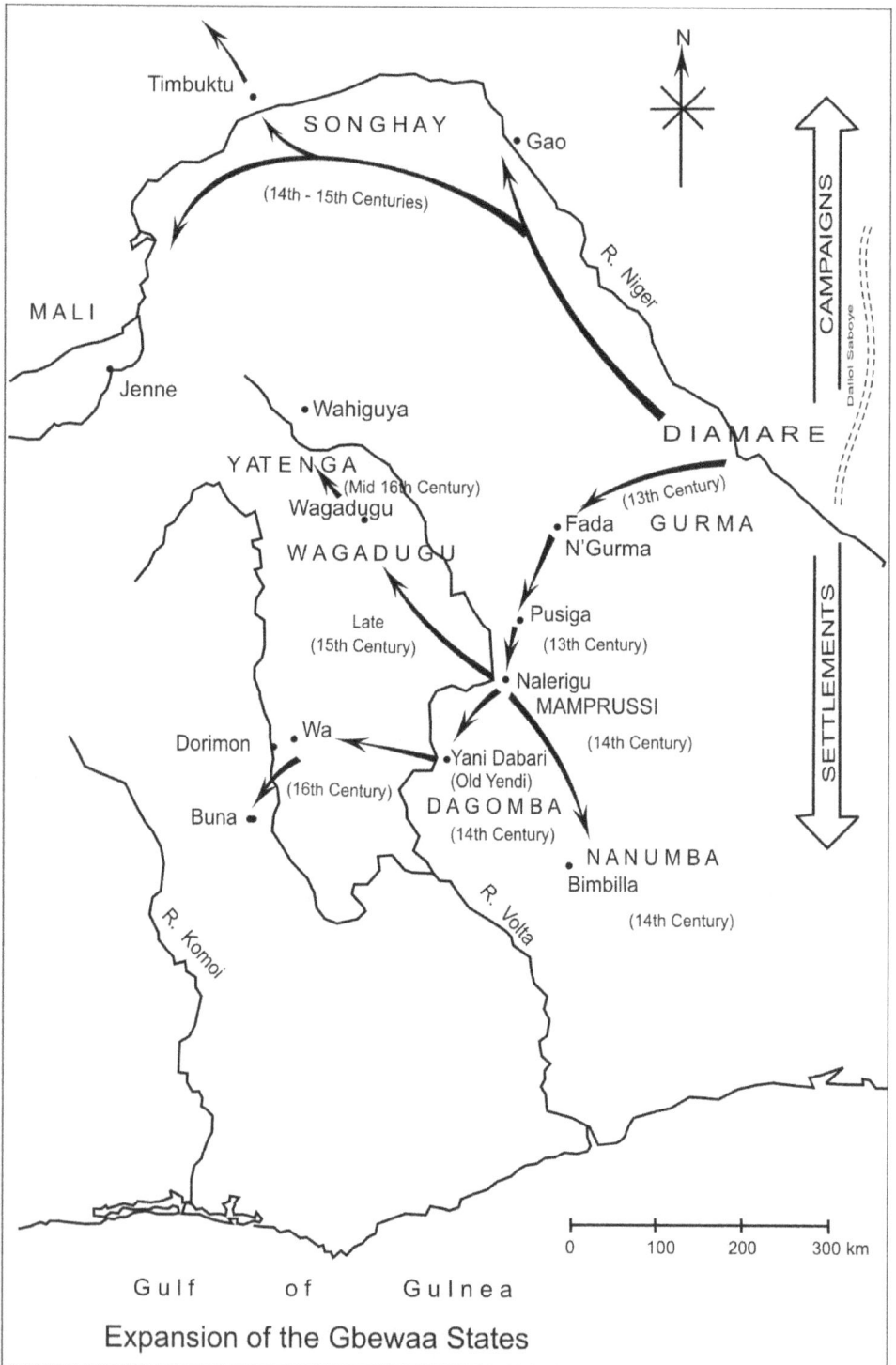

Fig. 3

CHAPTER THREE

DAGBON KINGDOM

Yaa Naa Mahamadu Abdulai IV (1969 – 1974)

Yaa Naa Yakubu Andani II (1974 – 2002)

YAA NAA ABUBAKARI MAHAMA 11 18ᵀᴴ JANUARY 2019 TO ....

3.0 DAGBON KINGDOM UNDER NAA NYAGSI (1416 – 1432)

After the division at Bagli, Naa Nyagsi (the Founder of Dagbon Kingdom) went back to Yani-dabari (Old Yendi). He first conquered Lingbung. It is for this reason they praise the people of Lingbung as "Lingbung Tuu Zabli" meaning, "He used Lingbung as the first point of fight". From Lingbung, Gaa "Gaa Lana Tuuveilga" was the next community, followed by Dipali, Zoosali, Signa, to the paramount princes' skin. For the paramount princes'skin, first was Zugu, Zangbaleng, to Vohu. Zugu chief was the head of chiefs in the Toma area, followed by Zangbaleng Naa and Vo-Naa. It was at Zugu that Naa Nyagsi started expanding chieftainship by enskining

33

opinion leaders as chiefs. This is to say, powerful Tindaanba were killed, and opinion leaders enskinned as chiefs. As such, Zugu is the elder skin in the Toma area (Western Dagbon). War captives were incorporated into the society. After Naa Nyagsi, Tampion and other communities such as Mion (Saanbu), Yelizoli, Zabzugu etc. came into existence. Naa Nyagsi ruled Dgbon for 16 years (1416 – 1432) according to oral traditional tree. Naa Nyagsi had his own children who became chiefs in Dagbon kingdom.

3.1 Yani Chiefs (Yaa Nanima)

After Naa Nyagsi, the next king was his regent 'Zulande Gmarigu,' who remained on the skin as Yaa Naa. Naa Zulande Gmarigu ruled Dagbon for 10 years (1432 – 1442), according to oral traditional tree. In a similar vein Naa Zulande Gmarigu regent "Na logu" also remained on the skin. After Zuu Na logu, Naa Dalgu (Datorili) was the next Yaa Naa, followed by Burigu ŋmumda. Naa Burigu ŋmumda's mother was a Konkomba woman. Konkombas came to Dagbon in the olden days and were regarded as settlers. They do not own any Land, not even Saboba that they claim to be their land. Later he went to visit his maternal uncles and realized that they should no more be recognized as Konkombas. It was there he enskinned the elder son named Sabani as Demong Naa. Sabani started the Demong skin. Demong Naa Sabani was killed and Yaa Naa Burigu ŋmumda again enskinned the second son Demong Naa Beziemkpana, who was also killed. Naa Burigu ŋmumda said, "As I promised to promote you my uncles, I still stand by it". He enskinned the third son, Demong Naa Denkurugu. Demong was originally called Namangbani. The meaning of Demong is "you ate food and left me". In Dagbani, its stands for "Din-mong" and the skin name/title is "Din-mong Naa-yili". Demong Naa Denkurugu was the one sitting on Demong skin when the father "Yaa Naa Burigu ŋmumda" died. He was enskinned as the regent. From this experience, the third born of Yaa Naa Burigu ŋmumda succeeded and became the regent, that gives meaning to the saying "it is the lucky one who becomes the regent and not necessarily the first son of a chief" as Kingdomd by oral tradition.

Naa Zolgu succeeded the skin after Naa Burigu ŋmumda. After Naa Zolgu, the regent Naa Zoŋ-bila (Zuu Zoŋ), who was praised or appellate as follows; "Da Warita Nabra, Zoŋ ŋmaya Ku Shi Mia, Taan Yolgu ni boli Zona" the meanings are as follows "a splitting wood increases in number, a crack wall cannot be sowed by a tread and Shea Trees will attract Bats" succeeded and remained on the skin. After Naa Zoŋ-bila, Ningmitooni was next on the skin, followed by Naa Dimani. He was the one who introduced butchering into Dagbon and later sprung to the other two Gbewaa sister Kingdoms. He acquired the butchering skills from Hausa people in Nigeria. Most Butchers in Dagbon, Nanunŋ and Mamprugu are descendants of Naa Dimani. The name Dimani implies; he used power to succeed the skin and that was exactly so. Naa Yenzoo succeeded the skin followed by Naa Dariziegu. After Naa Dariziegu, Naa Luro (son of Naa Zolgu) was next on the skin. Naa Luro regent (Zuu Titugri) also remained on the skin as Yaa Naa. It was then the Gonjas mobilized forces to attack Naa Titugri with the reason being that there is confusion among Dagbon chiefs and for that matter when they attack Naa Titugri, the other chiefs will not support him in the fight. As such, their chances of conquering him will be high and if they conquer him, it means they have conquered the whole Dagbon. Indeed, they attacked Naa Titugri (Zuu Titugri) and no chief from Dagbon supported him in the fight against the Gonjas. Until Bimbilla Naa sent tropes to help him fight them, off. From then Yani was moved from Yani-Dabari to the current Yendi, based on the advice from Bimbilla Naa to settle closer to him so that he can easily give him support when the need arises, because you are far away from me. Bimbilla Naa indicated to him that, he has conquered his side, and no one can attempt him. Naa Titugri (Zuu Titugri) was the one who moved Yani from Yani-Dabari to the current Yani (Yendi).

When he moved to the current Yani, Bimbilla Naa felt the land was too small for him and gave the current mion (Saambu) and Kpabya area to Naa Titugri and he enskinned his younger brother 'Voli' as Mion Lana. Hence, Mion Lana Voli was the first chief of Mion in Dagbon. The original mion is the one in Jagbuni area of Nanung skin land. The current mion and Kpabya area was owned by the Jagbuni chief. Other lands Bimbilla Naa released to Naa Titugri included Zabzugu area, Nakpali, the current Demonayili and Saboba areas. Naa Gmantambu (Nanung) was sharing boundary with Basaris in the Eastern Corridor of Northern region of Ghana and the Republic of Togo. Some writers claimed that Yaa Naa conquered Konkombas and took control as well as ownership of the current Yendi area is just a misconception or blind Kingdomment and should be regarded as a very big fallacy. It is nothing but a calculated lie to claim a land by a certain ethnic group. Bimbilla Naa (Naa Gmantambu) who came to meet Nanumbas and Nawuris originally owned the area.

Naa Zagli who was also the male son of Naa Luro succeeded Zuu Titugri. After Naa Zagli, Naa Zokuli (also son of Naa Luro) was next on the skin. His appellations were "Gmaligi-magna, Zori Kuli Ku Peni Zu u-kpuni" meaning: "Turning point and those who fear funerals will not have their hair skinned". His real name was Dawuni. After Naa Zokuli, Naa Gungobli was next. He used Yemo-karaga title to Yani. After Naa Gungobli, Naa Zangina succeeded him by the rule of appellations at Mamprugu. The rule of the game was the one who will give good titles/appellations, will become Yaa Naa. Elders of Mamprugu reminded the then Mamprugu chief about the Bagli day issue. Because on that remarkable day at Bagli, the three main founders (Tohagu, Gmantambu and Nyagsi) took an oath of succession after they shared their father's property and insignia that, any of us shall not and will never, forever enskin the other no matter the circumstances. Hence there is no day Yaa Naa can enskin Bimbilla Naa neither Nayiri nor the vice versa. It was for this reason Nayiri adopted the rule of appellation and Naa Zangina was able to give good appellations and succeeded Naa Gungobli. Naa Zangina was the son of Naa Titugri. He ruled Dagbon for 18 years (1700 – 1718). Some of his appellations were: "Nyagu Din-yelinma ni dei Bobri, Gunguma Tigsi Yeliya Kubang Kpema" meaning; "a person with broad chest fits for more dressing, it is difficult to determine the age of cotton fruits from Kapok Tree".

The following Sub-chiefs were provoked because of their disqualification by the rule of appellation; they cursed and placed a ban on their titles not to ever contest for the Yani skin (Yaa Naa title). Rather, they should remain in those titles and enjoy equal skin facilities. These titles include Yelizoli, Sunson, Tong, Kpu u, Warivi and Gundowagri. Those who occupied these skins or titles are sons and grandsons of Yaa Naa. Apart from the then Tong Lana Vubga who was a grandson of Naa Zolgu, the rest were sons of Naa Titugri

(Zuu Titugri). The above-mentioned titles previously could aspire to Yani skin, until the Mamprugu appellation day that brought about the curse and a ban of these titles or skins not to ever contest for Yani Skin. It has remained the same today.

Naa Andani Sigli was the son of Naa Zagli who succeeded Naa Zangina. He succeeded Naa Zangina because of fighting Golingolin Kumpatia "a Gonja chief who came to fight Naa Zangina and Dagombas in general". Again, sub-chiefs of Dagbon sat behind, said Naa Zangina should manover his way to fight Golingolin Kumpatia as he did at Mamprugu, and became Yaa Naa. Then Naa Zangina prepared well for the war and handed over the fight to Andani Sigli. He reminded Andani Sigli about the good appellations that he gave at Mamprugu "Nogali-muni Kunbang Naani, Savi Suma ni La am Kuriti and Zawuri-balgu ni La am Nobi i". So, he said go and fight Golingolin Kumpatia and you will succeed him for me. After me, you shall become the next Yaa Naa. By then Golingolin Kumpatia got closer to Sang and Andani Sigli met him at Sang Chirizan and indeed succeeded Golingolin Kumpatia. Golingolin Kumpatia wanted to take advantage of the chieftaincy struggle that brought confusion among Dagombas. Fortunately, Andani Sigli understood Naa Zangina and intervened. Hence, this brought about the Sang Chirizan war between Dagombas and Gonjas. Naa Andani Sigli ruled Dagbon for 20 years (1718 – 1738).

Naa Zangina's son, Zuu Jingli (Naa Binbiegu) was enskinned as the next Yaa Naa. It was during his term, Yani Princesses' brought confusion and the Yani Regalia was shared among the King Makers of Yani, otherwise it was kept at one place for Gushegu chief. Gushegu chief is the head of king makers in Dagbon Kingdom. Naa Binbiegu ruled Dagbon for 2 years (1738 – 1740). After Zuu Jingli (Naa Binbiegu), Naa Gariba was the next chief on Yani Skin. His appellation was "Sheigni Noo Tilgi Sulugu Kun Tilgi ŋo u" meaning "rainy season fowl is safe from Eagle and not from Fox". Naa Gariba came from the Yani Royal family both maternal and paternal. Oral tradition indicated that, the current Yani Royal family is made up of Abudus' and Andanis' who originated from Naa Zangina and Naa Gariba. Naa Gariba was the one who fought Ashantis'. It was at this war, the saying of "Kum Apim, Apim b ba ba fa wu". The sayings of "Kum Apim" were at two different levels in the history of Dagbon and Nanung. Naa Abarika I of Nanung also fought Anshantis' and the saying was "Kum Apim, Apim b ba". Naa Gariba ruled Dagbon for 5 years (1740 – 1745). Naa Saa-Lana Ziblim was next on Yani skin. He was the nephew of Naa Gariba and son of Naa Andan Sigli. His mother was Minara, a daughter of Naa Zangina. He ruled Dagbon for 18 years (1745 – 1763)

It is important to recall the Kingdom of confusion that occurred during the reign of Naa Gariba and Naa Saa-Lana Ziblim. Naa Saa-Lana Ziblim was fighting Naa Gariba spiritually when he was on Yani Skin as Yaa Naa. The spiritual fight led to the war between Naa Gariba and Ashantis. The Ashantis carried Naa Gariba away on their heads but could not kill him. When Naa Gariba was carried away, Naa Saa-Lana Ziblim applied force on Yani King Markers to enskin him as Yaa Naa. When Naa Gariba died, the elders of Dagbon could not perform the funeral of Naa Gariba. After the death of Naa Saa-Lana Ziblim, elders' of Dagbon came together and first performed the funeral of Naa Gariba, followed by Naa Saa-Lana Ziblim before the next Yaa Naa was enskinned. This very important experience could be employed to address the chieftaincy crisis that bedeviled Dagbon today.

Naa Ziblim Bandamda, (son of Naa Gariba) was enskinned after Naa Saa-Lana Ziblim. After him, Naa Andani (Naa Andan-Jangbariga), also son of Naa Gariba was next on the skin. Naa Ziblim Bandamda and Naa Andani appellations were "Ziblim ni o nyeli Andani, bi i gbani za yini la am mo ra, Ko kpubga za yini la am su, Soŋ bila za yini la am doonda, Dufeli za yini la am ta i" this means, "they gave birth to the two brothers in a week's interval. They were in the same room, sharing the same bathing facilities, mat and pillow and sucking the same breast milk". Bo u Paani Fantani gave birth to Naa Ziblim Bandamda and her room maid (Pa a-Bili u) gave birth to Naa Andan-Jangbariga in a week's interval.

Naa Koringa (Naa Mahami) son of Naa Ziblim Bandamda was next on the skin. After him was Naa Ziblim Kulunku. His appellations were as follows; "Kulunku la am kobga ku ŋmani paanga, Kinkambugli nambu dali ka sanlinsahi pun bi di puuni,

Nuzaa Buni Tebsa Nudirigu Yaa Zugu". He succeeded Yani from Kpatinga through a fight between him and Savelugu Naa Bukali Tampin Karagu, son of Naa Ziblim Bandamda, whose mother was a Gonja woman. After Naa Ziblim Kulunku succeeded him, he run with his people to the maternal side (Gonjas) and this resulted in war between Dagombas and Gonjas. Savelugu Naa Bukali Tampin Karagu's uncles could not take it and started preparing for the war. They include Wahipei Wura Belajapo, Singbe Wura Belajapo (Zom Gma Gmani). They were very powerful chiefs in Gonja Land. It was at this war that, Kunbung Naa Zakali and Yelzoli-Lana Yidaan-Togmah fought and conquered Gonjas and took away their Talking Drums to Kunbungu. The Talking Drums ever since remained in Kunbungu, which is a historic mark in Dagbon. Yelzoli-Lana Yidaan-Togmah was a powerful man in Dagbon; as such, he was ruling Nine (9) communities at the same period in the Kingdom of Dagbon. These communities were Zabzugu, Yelizoli, Demong, Nakpali (Korli), Nakpachia, Kunkon, Dagbon Gbungbalga just to mentioned some of the communities.

Naa Sumani (Naa Zoli) was the first son of Naa Koringa who the next chief on the skin was and again Naa Yakubu Nantoo I succeeded him through a fight. Naa Yakubu Nantoo was from Mion, because of confusion between him and Naa Sumani led to the fight. Naa Yakubu Nantoo ruled Dagbon for 25 years (1824 – 1849). After Naa Yakubu Nantoo, his regent (Naa Abdulai Nagbi u I) remained on the skin as Yaa Naa. Naa Abdulai Nagbi u was the one who went and fought Bassaris with the support of Nanumbas during the term of Bimbilla Naa Peinkpaa, who delegated Bakpaba Naa Iddrisah "the Regent of Bimbilla Naa Shero". Naa Abdulai Nagbi u ruled Dagbon for 27 years (1849 – 1876). Bakpaba Naa Iddrisah was the man of the war at Bassali. It was because of the effort of Bakpaba Naa Iddrisah that led to the victory of the Bassari war.

Naa Andani Jerilon II (Naani-goo) was next on Yani skin. It was during his term the royal gate of Yani was divided into Abudu and Andani gates. Naa Abdulai Nagbi u and Naa Andani Jerilon were all sons of Naa Yakubu Nantoo but different mothers. Naa Abdulai Nagbi u's mother came from Diari (Lami i) and he was praised as "Kanbang Pa a bia" whiles, Naa Andani Jerilon's mother came from Tampion (Galibang Budali). Napaga Lami i also gave birth to Sagnarigu Lana Sulemana. In this case, Sagnarigu Lana Sulemana and Naa Abdulai Nagbi u were the same mothers. Naa Andani Jerilon II ruled Dagbon for 23 years (1876 – 1899).

Naa Alhassan Tipariga was next on the skin after Naa Andani Jerilong. Naa Alhassan Tipariga was the son of Naa Abdulai Nagbi u and his mother (Memuna) came from Yani Kanbalayili. Coming from this background, he was praised as "Jingli Pa a bia", meaning, "he originated from Islamic family background". Naa Alhassan Tipariga ruled Dagbon for 17 years (1900 – 1917). After Naa Alhassan Tipariga, the next chief was Naa Abdulai Satanku li II (Naa Abudu Satanku li) who was the regent of Naa Alhassan Tipariga remained on the skin as Yaa Naa. His appellations were "Satanku li belim ku gma, Ziri dooi banŋ y limanŋli lana banŋ, Almunaafiki yi la aŋ kobga y nli lana yubu, Satanku li ba a ni Nong-kpani" meaning: "Satanic stone will never roll and get broken, no matter how you lie, the truth shall surface, and Satanic stone does not fear the stinger of Scorpion". His mother was called Gbanzaling or Saasi ili Asana. Naa Abdulai Satanku li II ruled Dagbon for 18 years (1920 – 1938). Naa Mahama Kpema II, son of Naa Andani Jerilong was the next Yaa Naa. His mother was called Naasikai. They appellate him as; "Suhu yini ba a ni dunia garibu, Dagbamba yoli y ligu Ka siliminga nya zaa" meaning: "faithfulness has no fear over temptations on earth, Dagombas have delayed in action and the Whiteman is firm on the ground". Naa Mahama Kpema II ruled Dagbon for 10 years (1938 – 1948). After him, was Naa Mahama Bila III. He was the son of Naa Alhassan Tipariga and his mother also came from Diari. As such, they appellate him as; "Kanbang pa a bia Mahama kurigu, Ziri nya sa malimali y limanŋli gari, Zamba lana d m kurugu ka nyina kabsi kpalin kuruguni and Su ulo buni din gbamda ku kpalin soli" meaning: "Lying is sweet but truth is best, something for patience even crawling shall never remain on the way". Naa Mahama Bila III ruled Dagbon for 5 years (1948 – 1953).

Naa Abdulai Gmariga III was the first son of Naa Mahama Bila III who remained on the skin as Yaa Naa after the funeral of his father was performed. His mother was called Gbanzalun Chimsi from Dagbon Gbungbalga. He was praised as; "Sagmarigon ku z ini tiŋa, ŋun zima ku tooi kuma na la ŋun baŋ-ma, Salnim ni za asi sheli ka Naa Wuni pihi maanda" meaning: "Ben sky shall never seat on the ground, the one who doesn't know me cannot kill me unless who knows me, what human rejects God cares for". Naa Abdulai Gmariga III ruled Dagbon for 13 years (1954 – 1967).

It was after the death of Naa Abdulai Gmariga, the Yani chieftaincy crisis started. There was a struggle for the regent of Naa Abdulai Gmariga (Naa Mahamadu) to remain on the skin. However, this could not materialize; finally, Naa Andani Zoli-Kugli III from Mion succeeded and became the next Yaa Naa after Naa Abdulai Gmariga. He ruled Dagbon for only Three (3) months (1968 – 1969). His appellations were "Manzobya Pa abia, Zoli Kugli din blinda ku kpalim saazu u" meaning, "a rolling stone from a mountain shall not remain on top". After Naa Andani Zoli-kugli, there was another chieftaincy struggle over the Yani Skin between the regent of Naa Abdulai Gmariga and Naa Andani Zoli-Kugli regent (Naa Yakubu Andani II). Upon several Governments interventions, the chieftaincy issue of Dagbon kept on re-occurring and has become a perpetual phenomenon. However, in order to straighten the chieftaincy succession record at this critical point and for the sake of peace, sanity, and chieftaincy development of Dagbon, we should go by the natural call to glory as follows.

Naa Mahamadu IV, the first son of Naa Abdulai Gmariga was the next Yaa Naa after Naa Andani Zoli-Kugli. His mother was called Gbanzalun Samata from Tolon. They appellate him as; "ŋun bibri zamba ku chirigi bi ri, Kul-noli din vi li ni la am nyuriba, Naa Wuni ni yuri so y la bi to malbu" meaning, "if you do not sabotage somebody, nobody will sabotage you, a river with plenty fish will attract more people and the one who god bless is always fortunate". Naa Mahamadu IV ruled Dagbon for 5 years (1969 – 1974). After him, Naa Yakubu Andani II, first son of Naa Andani Zoli-kugli was the next Yaa Naa. His mother was called Fatima, from Lengbung. Naa Yakubu appellations were "Tuuzabli Pa a-bia, dingambo Pa a-bia, Falwo li Pa a-bia" meaning, "son of Lengbung woman". Naa Yakubu Andani II ruled Dagbon for 28 years (1974 – 2002).

With the above records between Naa Mahamadu IV and Naa

Yakubu II, some people may not agree with it because it may not be in their interest. However, it should be respected as such to promote peace, unity, and development of Dagbon.

Yaa Naa Abubakari Mahama II is currently the overload of Dagbon after the Committee of Eminant Chiefs led by Asantehene Otumfuo Osei Tutu II mediated on the Dagbon Chieftaincy case. A roadmap was developed and implemented by the President Nana Addo Dankwa Akufo Addo in 2019. The roadmap settled on Yoo-Naa Abubakari Mahama to succeed the late Yaa Naa Yakubu Andani II. After the retual funeral "Nakuli" of the late Yaa Naa Yakubu Andani II, Yaa Naa Abubakari Mahama II was enskinned on the 18th of January 2019 as the successor and for that matter the current Yaa Naa of Dagbon.

YAA NAA ABUBAKARI MAHAMA 11 18TH JANUARY 2019 TO ....

3.2 Dagbon Kingdom Governance Structures and Systems

3.2.1 Dagbon Kingdom Council

Dagbon Kingdom Council is made up of the following titles.

1.	Yaa- Naa	13.	Kumbun-Naa
2.	Karaga –Naa	14.	Kuga-Naa
3.	Savelugu –Naa	15.	Zohi-Naa
4.	Mion-Lana	16.	Balo-Naa
5.	Kori-Naa	17.	Kum-Lana
6.	Demon-Naa	18.	Malle
7.	Gushie-Naa	19.	Bunga
8.	Yelzole-Lana	20.	Gagbin-Dana
9.	Gulkpe-Naa	21.	Kpahegu
10.	Nanton-Naa	22.	Gullana
11.	Sunson-Naa	23.	Chereponi Fame
12.	Tolon-Naa	24.	Tuguri-Nam

3.2.2 Dagbon Kingdom Judicial Council

The judicial council of Dagbon Kingdom comprises the following titles.

1.	Yaa-Naa (President)	7.	Gagbin-Dana
2.	Kuga-Naa (Vice President)	8.	Malle
3.	Zohi-Naa	9.	Kpahegu
4.	Balo-Naa	10.	Gullana
5.	Kum-Lana	11.	Tuguri-Nam
6.	Bunga		

3.2.3 Dagbon Traditional Council

In 1986 Dagbon Traditional Council was reviewed, as such the members comprises the following titles.

1.	Yaa-Naa (President)	16.	Tampion-Lana
2.	Mion-Lana	17.	Tijo-Naa
3.	Karaga-Naa	18.	Nyankpal-Lana
4.	Savelugu-Naa	19.	Tuguri-Nam

5.	Kuga-Naa (Vice President)	20.	Gomle
6.	Zohi-Naa	21.	Kpatia-Naa
7.	Gushie-Naa	22.	Namo-Naa
8.	Yelzole-Lana	23.	Chereponi Fame
9.	Gulkpe-Naa	24.	Saboba-Naa
10.	Nanton-Naa	25.	Nambili-Naa
11.	Sunson-Naa	26.	Sanguli-Naa
12.	Tolon-Naa	27.	Nafebi-Naa
13.	Kumbun-Naa	28.	Wonchigu-Naa
14.	Kori-Naa	29.	Sagnari-Naa
15.	Demon-Naa	30.	Pishegu-Lana

3.2.4 Elders' Titles in Dagbon

The elders' titles of Dagbon comprise the following titles.

1.	Gushiegu	11.	Yiziegu
2.	Kuga	12.	Kasuliyili
3.	Yelzole	13.	Gbulon
4.	Gulkpegu	14.	Dalun
5.	Nanton	15.	Zandua
6.	Sunson	16.	Langa
7.	Tolon	17.	Lungbun
8.	Kumbun	18.	Nyankpala
9.	Diare	19.	Salankpang
10.	Singa	20.	Woribogu

3.2.5 Titles for Priest

Bagli Naa

Namogu   Gbandari

Gushie Tindana   Lango u Tindana

Namburugu Tindana   Kparigu Tindana

Salaa Tindana   Safam Tindana

Yong Dooni Tindana   Tamalgu Tindana

Yong Dakpem Tindana   Zaankal Tindana

3.2.6 Titles for Queen Mothers

The Gbewaa Skin did not leave out daughters and granddaughters (Princesses) of Yaa-Naa in the distribution of titles and communities. Below are the titles.

1. Gundo-Naa
2. Kpatuya
3. Nakpanzoo
4. Kugulogu
5. Shilung
6. Yimahagu
7. Warigbani
8. Yiwogu
9. Fuyaa
10. Saasegile
11. Didoge

Gundogu is the top title in the hierarchy, followed by Kpatuya. As such, these two titles are strictly for daughters of Yaa-Naa. Granddaughters or any woman who are descendants of Yaa-Naa could occupy the rest of the titles.

*Figure 4 (Sketch Map Showing Major Towns
of Dagbon Kingdom)*

CHAPTER FOUR

NANUNG KINGDOM

Bimbilla Naa Natogmah Attah II (1944 – 1959)

Bimbilla Naa Dassana Abdulai (1959 – 1981)

Bimbilla Naa Abarika Attah II (1983 – 1999)

4.0 NANUNG KINGDOM UNDER NAA GMANTAMBU (1416 ....)

According to some writers, that Naa Gmantambu did not desert Naa Sitobu or his son Naa Nyagsi. It was rather Naa Nyagsi who pointed out "Doli Naa Nuu Zu u" to Naa Gmantambu the area he should establish his own Kindom. In addition, that marked the beginning of the name Nanumba. This is more a rumour than oral tradition source.

The ethnic name "Nanumba" is a corrupted Nawuri Kingdomment whenever Naa Gmantambu invites the Nawuris to a meeting in Bimbilla. They do make this Kingdomment in the ancient times; "Naa Nuba" meaning, "Go and hear and come". In those days, only few of the Nawuris could speak Dagbani/Nanunli, so those who understand the language were always chosen to attend meetings of Naa Gmantambu. After which they will go back home and passed the information to the others. The long stay of Nanumbas with Nawuris, as well as inter-marriages corrupted the original Dagbani that was spoken by the aboriginal Dagbamba to the present day Nanunli.

After the confusion at Bagli, Naa Gmantambu headed towards Yeji through Salaga to Attebubu. As at then Salaga and Yeji were not in existence. The only settlement was Attebubu with temporal structures such as thatch. From Attebubu, he went towards the east and settled at Nkonya-Bimbilla in the Volta Region. From Nkonya-Bimbilla, he came up North and finally settled at Shirikpamo, now called Bimbilla. Gmantambu first settled at Daalanyili. Daalana tried rejecting him, but he resisted. Kpandigli (male & female), Daalana, and Shirikpamo Tindaanba attempted fighting Gmantambu. All the young men fled and left the chief priests to seek refuge at Juo. Juo Nabang Tindana finally advised his colleagues that they cannot fight him and for that matter, they accepted Gmantambu by symbols of leaves signifying peace. We have accepted you and you must accept us said by Juo Nabang Tindana. Juo Nabang Tindana told Gmantambu my fellowships are Wumpigu Tindana as Tagnamo Naa, Gambugu Tindana, Lanjiri Tindana and Jilo Varili Tindana. Lanjiri initial settlement was at Nahabil Zoli (Lanjiri Tuyani) before and during the time of Naa Gmantambu after which the

50

community finally settled at the current Kukuo. Later in the night, Naa Gmantambu and Juo Nabang Tindana met and shared among themselves best cultural and traditional practices. This led to the final standardization of Bimbilla Chief's regalia/insignia by Naa Gmantambu and Juo Nabang Tindana currently referred to us as Juo Naa. It is for this reason Juo Naa became the head and only person to enskin or appoints Bimbilla Naa. He keeps the regalia/insignia and the regalia originated from Naa Gmantambu through the Gbewa skin to Juo Nabang Tindana now the Juo Naa.

Chichagi was not in existence before Naa Gmantambu came to Nanung. Chichagi originated from Naa Gmantambu, and it is the head of communities in the overseas apart from the Bassaris. Naa Gmantambu empowered Chichagi-Naa and entrusted the Oti River to him and it is for this reason Chichagi became one of the most senior communities. Korli (Nakpali) came into existance because of a man from Dagbon who was always with Chichagi Naa paying homage to Bimbilla Naa. The then Yaa –Naa enskinned the man as Kori-Naa at the request of Bimbilla Naa who offered the Kori-Naa land. The meaning of Kori-Naa is I am farming on the Chief's farm "Nkori-la Naa Puuni". That was Bimbilla Naa's Farm.

4.1 Nanung/Bimbilla Chiefs

Naa Gmantambu was the founder and for that matter first chief of Nanung. From Bagli, Naa Gmantambu went through Salaga, Yeji, and Atebubu to Nkunya Basabasa, Nkunya Wurinpong and Nkunya Bimbilla. He finally passed through Krachi, Kpandai and settled in Bimbilla. After, Naa Gmantambu, Naa Sulgme (the nephew of Naa Gmantambu) was the next chief of Bimbilla. However, I would like to give a brief explanation to Naa Sulgme before proceeding to the next chief of Bimbilla.

Naa Gmantambu was moving with his sister and her son. Naa Gmantambu was given birth to children, and none could survive except Kumkayo ri who grew up to a stage of young man. Finally, he also died at Daalanyili. Initially, Gbewaa's children did not know how to bury their cops; they either placed the corps on a tree or cover it on the ground with leaves, it was during the death of his son (Kumkayo ri), that he asked the Daalayili people to do what they do to their corps. They dug the grave in the form of a well and broadened the ground level very wide (the grave is locally called Silga). Naa Gmantambu was impressed and asked them to go ahead with the burial. After the burial, he requested to be buried same when he dies, and all his children/family should be buried same by the Daalanyili people. Hence, Naa Gmantambu instituted it that; every son of Bimbilla Skin should be buried the same way by the Daalanyili people, and this has been the tradition in present day Nanung.

After the burial of his son, he asked them to postpone the funeral, after the third day funeral rites until he dies before their funerals should be performed together as Bimbilla Naa so that, his son would be honoured as Bimbilla Naa. It is for this reason when every young prince die; he is given a title before burial such that he could be buried with the title and not with an ordinary name.

Naa Gmantambu cautions the elders of Nanung not to say he has no child. My nephew stands the chance to inherit me, and it is God who has given him that opportunity. His mother and I are the same sieveline. He indicated it by a demonstration; he cut his left hand with a Knife and that of the nephew's left hand for their blood to be mixed. He said, after I die, he should be made a regent and subsequently enskinned as Bimbilla Naa after you finish performing my funeral. Indeed, that was how Naa Sulgme became the second chief of Bimbilla.

Before Naa Gmantambu died, he moved from Daalanyili to Sirikpomo, which is the present day Bimbilla. Later, he decided to visit his brothers from Dagbon and on his way, he got to Dagbon Kpatinga, and his health condition was not favourable for him to proceed on the Juorney. He returned and died at Duuni. People did not physically bury Naa Gmantambu; also, he mysteriously entered the ground just like his father "Naa Gbewaa". A local round room was built around where he remained. According to the oral tradition, among Naa Gbewaa's children, Naa Gmantambu was the one who fought "Powerful Tindaanba" and passed away just like Naa Gbewaa.

According to the oral traditional records, Kumkayo ri was placed as the third chief, because he was honoured as Bimbilla Naa. The regent of Naa Sulgme known as Naa Dogiporigu was the fourth Bimbilla Naa. His appellation was "Dogiporigu ni shee turi". Meaning "a short man does not care about insults". The fifth Bimbilla Naa was Naa Badariga, and his appellation was "Badariga ku gmei-suli". The sixth Bimbilla Naa was Naa Na i Baarigu, followed by Naa Saa as the seventh chief of Bimbilla. The eighth chief of Bimbilla was Nakoŋa. It was during his enskinment as Bimbilla Naa Joeli skin started. That is, the elders insisted he could not use his name for the Bimbilla skin. As such, he has to get a title. He was enskinned as Joeli Naa after which he was honoured as Bimbilla Naa. Joeli (Zoli) in Nanungli Means "Mountain" and for that matter chief of mountain. Naa Kunbalinkulga was the ninth chief of Bimbilla. His appellation was "Benyi ira ku balim kulga, Danderi kun gbabi kurigu". Meaning "animals that flies will not beg a river to cross, ants will never bite a metal". The tenth Bimbilla chief was Naa Nyelinbolgu. He was praised as "Pa a balima". Meaning, "a pleading woman". In addition, he was the regent of Naa Kunbalinkulga and remained on the skin as Bimbilla. The eleventh chief of Bimbilla was Naa Wobgu (Naa Pampamli or Mahamuda), followed by Naa Saa Kpang as the twelve Bimbilla chief. He is also called Naa Damba. His appellation was "Saa kpani wurim tia kun wurim zoli". Meaning "a lighting storm can only destroy a tree and not a mountain". Naa Sulgu (Naa Maamani) succeeded Naa Damba and became the thirteenth chief of Bimbilla. He was from the Suburi family of Bimbilla and the regent of Naa Wobgu (Naa Pampamli or Mahamuda). Naa Gbuguma (Naa Azuma) also succeeded Naa Sulgu and became the fourteenth chief of Bimbilla. It was at this stage, the royal gate of Nanung was divided into Gbugumayili and Bang-yili to prevent future chieftaincy clashes on the Bimbilla skin. According to oral tradition, Naa Gbuguma ruled Nanung over 40 years. Both gates were made to take a succession oath with the skins and the Holy Quran facilitated by the first chief Imam in the person of Imam Mahama Walji. The chief Imam was a Hausa by tribe from Nigeria. They swore to rule/enskin as Bimbilla Naa one after the other and that no instance shall one particular gate rule/enskin on two consecutive times or more. In addition, no one from any of the royal gates shall use his name or any other title apart from Dakpam and Nakpa. It is highly prohibited to go against this traditional oath of succession to Bimbilla Skin/Title. Any attempt to bridge this oath of traditional eskinment, certainly will cause socio-cultural/economic havoc in the Nanung Kingdom. It should be highly respected and followed strictly. It has been adhered to ever since it was instituted.

According to Cliff S. Maasole, that, "a Dagomba man who settled at Kpalga was the one who introduced Islam to Nanung." This is a complete rumour than a fact. The first Imam of Bimbilla in the person of Chief Imam Mahama Walji was the one who introduced Islam to Nanung during the reign of Naa Gbuguma (Naa Azuma). The Chief Imam Mahama Walji was engaged in the Sahel Trans-Sahara trade from Nigeria to Ghana. The route was through Togo to Chichagi – Bimbilla and Bimbilla – Salaga road. He was doing cattle trade and Cola-nut. It was during the reign of Naa Sulgu that, he ordered some men in Bimbilla to kill his cattle on his way to the southern part of Ghana through the Chichagi and Bimbilla –Salaga road. The second batch of his cattle was killed in Bimbilla. Naa Sulgu succeeded Bimbilla Naa Damba through war and drove away Nakpa Naa Azuma and Dakpam Naa Kpanjogu. Dakpam Naa later came back preparing to fight Naa Sulgu. Fortunately, Dakpam Naa was linked up with Imam Mahama Walji, he supported Dakpam Naa Kpanjogu with spiritual means from the Holy Quran, and he succeeded Naa Sulgu in a war between Naa Sulgu and Dakpam Naa Kpanjogu. There Dakpam Naa Kpanjogu requested Imam Mahama Walji to remain in Bimbilla to help them rule Nanung very well. The family of Chief Imam Mahama Walji is the present-day chief Imam Royal gate of Bimbilla and occupying a whole area in Bimbilla called Lemam Fong. For more information, refer to History of the Gbewaa Kingdoms – Part II (Wars in the Gbewaa Kingdoms)

Naa Nyong (Naa Imoro) became the fifteenth chief of Bimbilla. His appellation was "Nyong din zibsi ku zali ŋmamli". He was the son of Naa Damba. He ruled Nanung for only one day and died. However, his death was not disclosed to the public, until 45 days it was officially announced by the elders. It is for this reason why when Bimbilla Naa passes away, not until three days; his funeral is not formally announced. Hence the death and secret burial of Naa Nyong marked the beginning. This is different in the case of

Yani and Mamprugu. For Yani, the funeral is formally announced immediately the Yaa Naa passes away and burial is performed with drumming and singing songs of praises.

After Naa Nyong, Naa Bulali-bila (Naa Kurugu-kpaa) was next on Bimbilla Skin as the Sixteenth chief of Bimbilla. Naa Bulali-bila is the younger brother of Bulali-kpeima all were children of Nakpa Naa Sanboni (younger brothers of Naa Gbuguma). The elders said, Bulali-kpeima you are the elder of the gate, so it is your term, he said, he is interested in Juo's Title and for that matter, the younger brother (Bulali-bila) can go for the Bimbilla Title. Indeed, Bulali-kpeima was enskinned as Juo Naa. He was the one who started the Juo Title, but that was his maternal side and was brought up from the maternal home (Juo). Juo was previously a Tindana Title (Nabang Tindana). After his enskinment, he moved to Jakpafili and later heard drumming in Bimbilla, then he asked his elders what was happening in Bimbilla? The elders said it was the enskinment of Bulali-bila as Bimbilla Naa. He said again this looks more serious and colourful than my enskinment. The elders responded, chief your enskinment and his cannot be the same. This is the reason why they appellate every Juo Naa as "Juo Naa duri gaa ni kpala pu isiri nam". Meaning "had I know is almost at last". During the term of Naa Kurugu, Nanumbas fought with Ashantis "Kanbon-balibali yuuni". Naa Abarika I (Naa Bang) was the seventeenth chief of Bimbilla. He fought the Ashantis on behalf of Naa Kurugu. He was holding Dakpam Title when he fought the Ashantis after which he became Bimbilla chief. His appellations were "Sankali bang baŋ balima ku lebgi salma bang, Nolo u di bori nuŋ valbu ka si a gari kobga". Meaning "a decorated silver bangle cannot turn to be gold bangle; a Cock intends to swallow a Scorpion but is cautious".

Naa Shero was next after Naa Abarika I and he became the eighteenth chief of Bimbilla. He was the son of Naa Gbuguma. His appellations were "ŋalim din vi li ni la im kperiba, Anzinfa to isi pi la ku gmani sanli, Wuu mana daa wura baŋdi dijesuli". Naa Natogmah (Naa Peinkpaa) was the nineteenth chief of Bimbilla. He was the regent of Naa Abarika. His appellations were "Peinkpaa virigbandi, Salma saa kuya ka ban zori wori zon-ba i bi daalobo" meaning; "a piercing metal will penetrate skins, gold rain is set and those who fear cold run

away and missed their wealth". Naa Kalo (Naa Mahama) was next
on the skin after Naa Peinkpaa, and he became the twentieth chief
of Bimbilla. He was the son of Naa Gbuguma. They appellate him
as; "Kalo din vi la ni gooi yabla" meaning; "a good thatch gate can
attract fish". After him was Naa Toli (Naa Dahamani) who became
twenty-one on Bimbilla skin. His appellation was "Toli din ka zibu
zoo blima" meaning; "a very big Mortar that cannot be carried on
the head will surely roll on the ground". Naa Toli was also the son of
Naa Abarika and even the same mother with Naa Peinkpaa.

Naa Yakubu Savigu (Savisuŋ ni la im kruti, Gampelisuŋ ni la m
niriba) became the twenty second chief of Bimbilla. However, there
was a very serious misunderstanding before Naa Yakubu Savigu was
enskinned. It came because of Bakpaba-Naa Iddrisa who wanted
to use Bakpaba's Title to Bimbilla when Nakpa-Naa was there.
Bakpaba-Naa Iddrisa was driven away because of conflict between
him and Naa Peinkpaa. The conflict arose when Naa Pienkpaa
prepared Bakpaba-Naa Iddrisa and sent him to support his brother
"Yaa Naa Abdulai Na ibiegu" in the fight against Baassaris. After
Bakpaba-Naa Iddrisa successfully fought for "Yaa Naa Abdulai
Na ibiegu" in Baassari's conflict, he was convinced that, he could
succeed Naa Peinkpaa and become Bimbilla Naa, which was not
possible. As a result, he went and settled around Krachi. Before he
returned to Bakpaba, his younger brothers from the Gbugumayili
gate had progressed to Nakpa. After the death of Naa Toli from
Bang-yili, Bakpaba-Naa Iddrisa wanted to use power over Nakpa-
Naa Yakubu Savigu. Juo Naa said "I could not give it to you because
there is an oath in Nakpa and Dakpam over Bimbilla succession".
Bakpaba-Naa Iddrisa said Juo Naa should prepare for an attack
if he is not going to be the one to be enskinned. The very day Juo
Naa scheduled for the enskinment of Naa Yakubu Savigu could
not come on because Bakpaba-Naa Iddrisa threatened to attack. A
meeting was summoned by Juo Naa to inform the elders of Nanung
the reason why the enskinment could not come on. Dakpam Naa
Bukari said, is it true Bakpaba-Naa Iddrisa, you actually said it? The
answer was yes by Bkpaba-Naa Iddrisa. Nba Juo Naa gets prepared
tonight to do your work (enskinment of Bimbilla Naa), "Bakpaba-
Naa Iddrisa prepare very well, we shall see who who is" said
Dakpam Naa Bukari (regent of Naa Peinkpaa). Indeed, Naa Yakubu

was enskinned successfully without any interference by Bakpaba-Naa Iddrisa. Again, Bakpaba-Naa Iddrisa went back to Krachi area, Banda to be precise and as such the founder of the present-day Banda community in the Kpandai District. Some few months after the enskinment of Naa Yakubu Savigu, Bakpaba-Naa Iddrisa came back vigorously with a war and killed Naa Yakubu Savigu. Dakpam Naa Bukari said, he would never call Bakpaba-Naa Iddrisa his father (Bimbilla Naa). He also prepared and attacked Backpaba-Naa Iddrisa and killed him around Kpatinga area specifically known as walinpaw-ni. The magical death of Bakpaba-Naa Iddrisa has given rise to the existence of two Gods; "Chebto ancient pots & Shrine and Pinaa Shrine & Cave". These historic landmarks are very important sites for tourism development.

After Dakpam Naa Bukari killed Bakpaba-Naa Iddrisa, it was the turn of Dakpam Naa Bukari to be enskinned as Bimbilla Naa. He said, "I would not seat on this burnt and smoking skins of Bimbilla". As such, he has whole heartedly given this chance to the Uncle Naa Wahu who was the then Chamba Naa. Juo Naa said even though you have openly given this chance to your uncle, but it will still go against the oath of Bimbilla skin succession. Dakpam Naa Bukari still insisted it should be given to his uncle and Juo Naa said then do it yourself, because I will not do it to cause a problem for the people of Juo. After proper understanding was reached, Naa Wahu was enskinned as Bimbilla Naa, and he was the twenty-third chief of Bimbilla.

The Nanumba and German war occurred during the term of Naa Wahu in 1898. Naa Wahu ruled Nanung for 35 years (1890 – 1925). Naa Wahu appellations were "Kundung Kurili lukpaha ka kundung bihi wari waa, Lamihi dapali ban ka izali ni gurigi, Abarika dapali ban ti su a ni mei-ya, Daku u din daŋ duu ni kari wori", meaning; "old wolf falls sick, and the young ones are dancing, those who prepared would be disorganized, those erected thatch structures, will build houses and the first fuel wood that enters the room will prevent cold".

Naa Ziblim Kuntibsa was the twenty-fourth chief of Bimbilla, followed by Naa Mahami who the twenty-fifth chief of Bimbilla was.

Naa Salifu should have been the twenty-fifth chief of Bimbilla, but he was arrested and detained by the Germans due to certain issues. When they arrested Naa Salifu and detained him at Krachi, the German Governor asked for the one who was next to Naa Salifu, to be enskinned. Naa Mahami was the one next to him from Gbungbalga. This means it was still the turn for Naa Bang-yili and there was no interference from Gbugumayili. After Naa Mahami, Naa Haruna was next on the skin of Bimbilla as the twenty-sixth chief. However, there was a problem here to. By then, the Germans were governing the eastern corridor previously known as the Transvolta Togo land. They were based in Krachi and sent a delegation to witness the performance of Bimbilla Naa Mahami's funeral. Before they started the funeral, they sent for the then Nakpa Naa and he refused. After the funeral, again, they sent for the Nakpa Naa with some of the German Governor delegation and again he refused. The German Governor asked the elders who represented the Nakpa Naa and performed the funeral. The elders said Bakpaba-Naa Haruna, and the Governor said he should be enskinned as Bimbilla Naa. Juo Naa resisted and said he does not want to go against the Bimbilla succession oath. The Governor asked Bakpaba-Naa Haruna what instructions your elder brother (Nakpa Naa) gave to you. He said that I should do all what is necessary on his behalf. It was finally resolved that, Bakpaba-Naa Haruna should be given the nod on behalf of his elder brother "Nakpa Naa" and that at any point his elder brother expressed interest, he should hand over to him. This was how Bakpaba-Naa Haruna used Bakpaba title to Bimbilla skin.

After Naa Haruna, Naa Salifu was returned to the skin of Bimbilla based upon consultation with the then Dakpam Naa Attah who openly obliged Naa Salifu to come and continue. After he was released by the Germans from detention at Krachi. Naa Salifu was the twenty-seventh chief of Bimbilla as such, they appellate him as "Nama sagkurili, Naŋu ni min di nam ka zang zali beigni nla i di".

Naa Abdulai Kurugu-kpaa was next on the skin of Bimbilla and he was the twenty-eighth chief of Bimbilla. Naa Abdulai Kurugu-Kpaa ruled Nanung for 18 years (1926 – 1944). After Naa Abdulai Kurugu-kpaa, Naa Natogmah II was the twenty-ninth chief of Bimbilla. Dakpam Naa Dadikai missed Bimbilla skin shortly within some few days by death. Naa Natogmah had the opportunity and used Gbungbalga title to Bimbilla skins. He ruled Nanung for 15 years (1944 – 1959)

Naa Dassana became the thirtieth chief of Bimbilla. There was another misunderstanding between Nakpa Naa Dassana and Bakpaba-Naa Dawuni. That is, Bakpaba-Naa Dawuni claimed that, by birth he was the elder person in Gbugumayili gate, whiles Nakpa Naa Dassana by chieftaincy title was the senior most in the gate. It resolved that, there is an oath of succession to Bimbilla skin for Nakpa and Dakpam titles only. With this, Nakpa Naa is the one who qualifies to be enskinned as the Bimbilla Naa. After Naa Dassana was enskinned, he gave Nakpa title to Bakpaba-Naa Dawuni and Bakpaba title to the regent of Naa Natogmah. The Bakpaba title was a misplaced title for the regent of Naa Natogmah II, because it is not the Naa Bag-yili titles which has never happened according to the custom and tradition of Nanung. Naa Dassana ruled Nanung for 22 years (1959 – 1981). His appellation was "Gbungbun turi babli dabayi babli beliya".

Naa Abarika Attah II was the thirty-one chiefs of Bimbilla. History has repeated in the Naa Bang-yili royal gate. Naa Natogmah II and Naa Abarika II were the same mother and the same father like in the case of Naa Pienkpaa and Naa Toli. This is a unique historic event in Naa Bang-yili and Nanung. It has never happened in Dagbon or Mamprugu. Naa Abarika II ruled Nanung for 16 years (1983 – 1999). Naa Abarika appellations were "Gbanbeigu, so yipri so yo im mo" meaning; "a strong skin, you will disturb it and leave it, if somebody misbehave him/her was influenced by another person".

4.2 Nanung Kingdom Governance Structures and Systems

4.2.1 Nanumba Traditional Council

The Nanumba Traditional Council is made of the following members:

Bimbilla Naa – President
Juo Naa – Vice President

Gambuga Naa
Dakpam Naa & Nakpa Naa
Lanjiri Naa
Jilo Naa
Chichagi Naa
Debsi Naa
Wulensi Naa
Suburi Naa
Kpihibara Naa
Worikpamo
Tolon Naa
Jua Naa
Bakpaba Naa
Chamba Naa
Gbungbalga Naa
Kpatihi-Naa is a co-opted member.

4.2.2 Council of Elders

The Council of Elders is made up of the following members:
Kpihibara Naa
Suburi Naa
Worikpamo
Kpihiga Naa
Tamalgu
Bomaha-Naa
Yimaha-Naa
Zayuri-Naa
Bripeil-Naa
Nbamali
Kpatihi-Naa

4.2.3 Rotational Gate System of Nanung Kingdom

The Nanung Kingdom has two royal gate system titles of succession to the highst skin title known as Bimbilla Skin. They are, Gbugumayili and Bang-yili gate system titles. Below is a presentation of the two rotational gate system titles:

4.2.3.1 Gbuguma-yili Royal Gate Titles.

Title	Village/Town
Nakpaa – Naa Most Senior Title	Nakpaa
Bakpaba – Naa Second Senior Title	Bakpaba
Karaga – Lana	Kalgah
Jua – Naa	Jua
Lepusi– Naa	Lepuhi
Gundow – Naa	Gundoo
Lanja – Naa	Langja
Boyu – Naa	Makayili
Yayiri – Lana	Yayiriya
Nating – Lana	Natiŋa
Banvim – Lana	Banvim
Suya – Naa	Kabulya
Yamo	Yamo
Mion.	Mion/Jagbuni

Nakpa and Bakpaba follow each other in terms of seniority; the rest of the titles beginning from Karaga can overlap each other in succession to Bakpaba and Nakpa. In addition, if a male son from the Gbugumayili gate is holding Lanja title, he can aspire to other titles such as Lepusi-Naa, Jua-Naa, Gundow-Naa, Bakpaba-Naa and Nakpa-Naa. However, if a female son or an ordinary person is holding the Lanja title, he cannot aspire to any of the above-mentioned titles. Female sons or ordinary persons are strictly limited to Lanja.

Yamo and Mion are old communities and for that, matter titles since Naa Gmantambu came to Nanung. New communities had progressed over them repeatedly, making these communities/titles to remain backwards in succession and progression. These communities/titles eventually became titles for elders in the Gbugumayili gate and can no longer aspire to other titles.

4.2.3.2 Bang-yili Royal Gate Titles.

Title	Village/Town
Dakpam-Naa; Most Senior	Dakpam
Chamba-Naa; Second	Chamba
Gbungbalga-Naa; Third	Gbumgbalga
Lungni-Naa	Lungni
Sakpe-Naa	Sakpe
Gimam-Naa	Jimam
Tuu-Naa	Tuu
Kukuo-Naa	Nassamba-Kukuo
Kpaluhi-Naa	Kpaluhi
Sikpam-Naa	Sikpam
Nassamba-Naa	Nasamba
Chirifa –Naa	Chirifa

From Gbungbalga, the rest of the titles can also overlap each other to the three senior titles. Chirifa is one of the oldest community/titles. Due to succession and progression by some of the new communities/titles, it has remained back and now regarded as elders title. Previously, with Chirifa title you could aspire to other titles.

4.2.4 Elders / King Makers of Bimbilla Skin (Salaa Kpamba)

Juo-Naa (head of King Makers)
Tagnamo-Naa
Gambuga-Naa
Lanjiri-Naa
Chichagi-Naa

Sirikpamo-Tindana
Jilo-Naa

Wulensi Naa was recently added to the elders. Otherwise, Wulensi Naa is a title for the Priest. Another important issue concerning the elders; refers to us, as king makers is the Substitution of Joeli for Tagnamo. The reason of this substitution came because of Tagnamo title being transferred to Dagbon because, Dagbon was the paternal side of the then Tagnamo Naa who went back to Dagbon with the Tagnamo title. The Tagnamo Naa was in Tagnamo, served his maternal uncles, and became the most elderly person among them. When Tagnamo title became vacant, they agreed for him to go for the title. Indeed, when he went in for the title, after which he returned to Dagbon with the Tagnamo title and said, "when you go to your maternal home and get promoted, you have to go back to your paternal home with the promotion".

Tagnamo title is not lost; the male children stand the chance to retrieve the title back to Nanung because Tagnamo is Nanung skin land.

Kpatihi-Naa is not a core member of the King Makers but a co-opted member, who performs delegator's function by Gambuga-Naa and Lanjiri-Naa; by putting the insignia on the appointed Bimbilla Naa by Juo-Naa.

4.2.5 PRIEST

Daalana
Kpandi ili
Kpandi ili Poonaa
Wulensi – Naa
Duuni Lana among others

4.2.6 QUEEN MOTHERS

4.2.6.1 Bang-yili:

Kpaliga Ponaa
Nakpanzou Naa

4.2.6.2 Gbugumayili:

Gikuhi Ponaa
Ku logu Lana
Shilin Naa
Kpatuya

Debsi title is for both Bang-yili and Gbugumayili royal gates. Suburi was a title for the Bimbilla royal gate, until when it became a title for the elders. After Naa Sulgu from the Suburi gate, the title became elders' title due to a ban that marked the beginning of the Gbugumayili and Bang-yili royal gates. Otherwise, Suburi title previously could aspire to Bimbilla title/skin.

Previously, Nanung had titles for chief's wives until the reign of Naa Mahama Kalo; it ceases to exist in Nanung or Bimbilla skin. After Naa Pienkpaa who gave titles to his wives, Naa Mahama Kalo was next and did not give titles to his wives, and eventually this ceased to exist in Nanung or Bimbilla skin.

Titles for both Bang-yili and Gbugumayili royal gates are strictly for members from royal gates and not for sons of females from both gates, neither person outside the two gates. It does not limit it to only sons of Bimbilla Naa, but grandsons and even great grandsons qualify for any of the titles from both royal gates that can aspire to Bimbilla Naa's title. Dagbon Yani (Yaa Naa) and Mamprugu Nayiri titles are limited to only sons of Yaa Naa and Nayiri not in the case of Nanung or Bimbilla title.

4.2.7 Functions of Kingmakers

The primary role of the Kingmakers is to enskin a Bimbilla Naa whenever the Bimbilla skin title becomes vacant. These revered chiefs play various roles in the enskinment process such as:

- Selection of the candidate: This is done by the Juo Naa as Head of the

Kingmakers. He consults the Deities and gods of the Nanung land through soothsayers to reveal the most suitable candidate to him. He then informs the other Kingmakers about the revelation he has received and ask for their opinion on the candidate revealed to him and whom he has chosen. These other Kingmakers may comment on his choice but cannot enforce what they want.

- Presentation of cola nuts to the selected candidate to notify him of his elevation to the high and coveted office of Bimbilla Naa (Overload of Nanung). Juo Naa can ask any of the Kingmakers to perform this function.
- Escort of the to-be Bimbilla Naa to meet the Juo Naa at a secret location in the palace of the deceased Bimbilla Naa. This function is performed by the Langiri Naa and Gambugu Naa.
- Cleansing or bathing of the to-be Bimbilla Naa with herbal bath prepared by Juo Naa. This role is played by the Langiri Naa and Gambugu Naa under the supervision of Juo Naa.
- Standing guard at the location where these customary rites are performed on the prospective Bimbilla Naa. This is to ward off any intruders. The Guard duty is performed by the Jilo Naa, Chichagi Naa, Juali Naa and Dibsi Naa.
- Enrobement of the prospective Bimbilla Naa with the sacred regalia. This role is played by the Kpatihi Naa on the instruction of the Juo Naa.

4.2.7.1 Their specific roles/functions of the kingmakers are:

4.2.7.2 Juo-Naa:

Is the chairman of kingmakers of Nanung. According to the custom and tradition of Nanung, Juo Naa is responsible for the following:

- Head of kingmakers responsible for the selection of Bimbilla Naa.
- Vice president of the Nanumba Traditional Council.
- He receives Reigns of Power "Kpanjogu" from the Regent of the deceased Bimbilla Naa and his uncles, aunties, and sisters.
- Head of Tindamba in Nanung.

- Custodian of the regalia.
- He is a principal signatory at the traditional council level for the gazette of Bimbilla Naa to confirm that the enskinned Bimbilla Naa was validly selected by him as head of kingmakers.
- He is the grandfather of Nanung kingdom and gives Bimbilla Naa "Yaan-laɣfu", literary meaning token for grandchildren, during Fire Festivals.

These powers make Juo Naa the principal authority for the selection and enskinment of the Bimbilla Naa.

4.2.7.3 Gambuga-Naa:

He is next to Juo-Naa and for that matter second in command. Gambuga-Naa is responsible for the following:

- Gambuga-Naa is the custodian for the Red Fist.
- He put the Red Fist on the selected Bimbilla-Naa after the regalia during the enskinment of Bimbilla-Naa.
- He is consulted by Juo-Naa during the selection of the Bimbilla-Naa.

4.2.7.4 Lanjiri-Naa:

He is third in command and performs delegated functions during the selection and enskinment of Bimbilla-Naa. In addition, he does the following:

- He notifies the selected candidate by presenting him with cola nuts. The Kpatihi Naa accompanies him to do the presentation.
- He escorts the Bimbilla Naa selected to the old palace of the late Bimbilla-Naa for enskinment rites to be performed with the assistance of Kpatihi-Naa.
- He also escorts the newly enskinned Bimbilla-Naa back to his home for confinement and takes care of him for seven days while he is in confinement.

These three kingmakers listed above are core in the selection and enskinment process of the Bimbilla Naa. The rest of the members namely, Chichagi-Naa, Jilo-Naa, Juali-Naa, Wulehi-Naa and Debsi-Naa play consultative roles during the selection of Bimbilla-Naa. The Wulehi Naa performs post enskinment rites (He is the first to perform cultural dance at the newly enskinned Bimbilla Naa palace before another chief or group of persons can perform cultural dance at the palace). The Kpatihi Naa serves as an errand person to the other kingmakers and also stays with the newly enskinned Bimbilla Naa during his confinement as part of the enskinment process.

4.3

NANUNG STATE

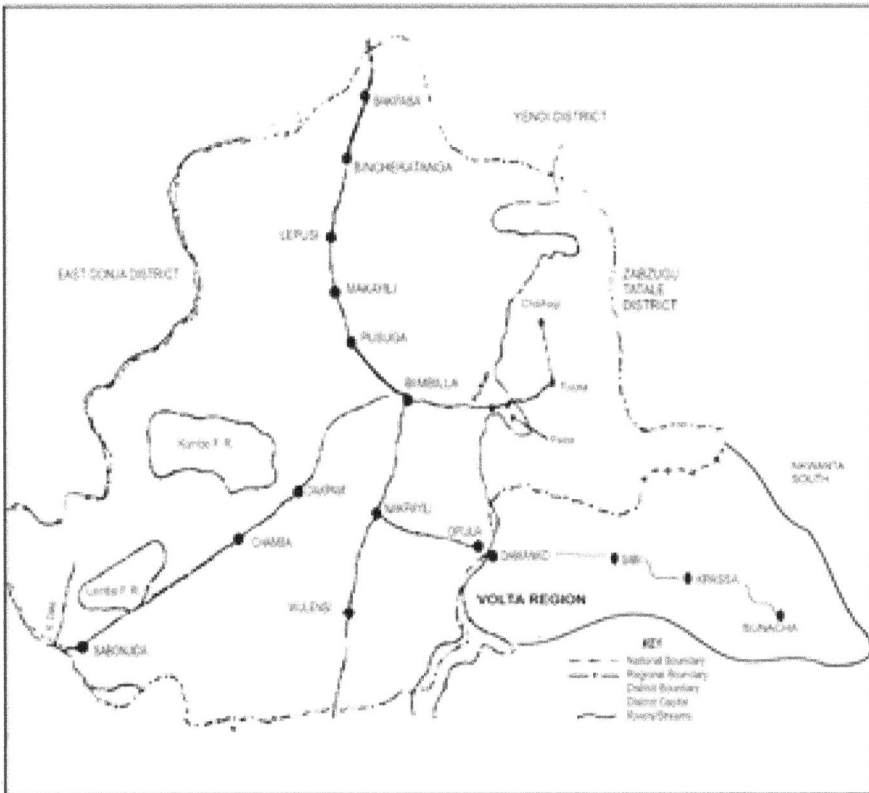

A Sketch Map Showing NANUNG

Fig. 5

Fig. 5 (A Sketch Map Showing Nanung)

4.4 The Disputed Kpassa Land Area Boundary Settlement.

IN THE STOOL LANDS BOUNDARIS SETTLEMENT COMMISSION SITTING AT THE MEETING ROOM 4, STATE HOUSE ACCRA TUESDAY, 25TH DAY OF SEPTEMBER 1979, <u>BEFORE MR J. K. ESSIEM, DEPUTY COMMISSIONER</u>.

**Enquiry No.
13/75**

IN THE MATTER OF BOUNDARY DIDPUTE BETWEEN

NANUMBA (N. R.)

SHIARE (V. R.)

<u>JUDGMENT:</u>

This matter was refferred to this Commission by the Court of Appeal in Civil Appeal No. 4 of 1976. The relevant part of the order of the Court of Appeal was as follows:

"This case is remitted to the Stool.
Land Boundaries Settlement Commission to determine the earstern boundary of the land over which the skin of Nanumba has proprietory of jurisdictional interest."

It is therefore, with the Eastern boundary of the Nanumba Skin Lands that we are concerned in this enquiry.

The case of the Nanumba is that their lands extend beyond the Oti River and include the lands general known as Kpassa Lands. From their claims, the Kpassa Lands marks their eastern boundary.

The Atweodes on the other hand claimed that: The River Oti was the boundary between Nanumbas and the Atweodes. The Kpassa Lands, they claimed belonged to the Atweode Traditional Area.

68

The eastern boundary of the Nanumba Skin Lands, as claimed by the Nanumbas, was set out in paragraph II their Amended Statement of claim filed on 15/9/1977, it is as follows:

"Thus, the Nanumba Skin Lands form on the right, or eastern side of the herin before described line with lands of the following,

    a. In the north and towards the north-east with Dagomba.
    b. In the north-east with Togo.
    c. In the east and the towards south-east with the Challa.
    d. In the south-east through south to south-west with the Gonja.

In support of this claim they called four (4) witnesses. Their evidence establishes one thing clearly and that is that the Gonjas, the Dagombas and the Challas are adjoining boundary owners in the area involved in this enquiry.

The first witness for the Nanumbas was Charibo Na Kpebo. He is a Nanumba resident at Kpassa. He gave evidence as to the boundaries claimed by the Nanumbas. Concerning their boundary with the Shiare or Atweode Traditional Area, he stated that the Nanumbas did not share boundary with the Atweodes but with the Challas. His evidence names the Gonjas, the Dagombas and the Challas as the adjoining boundary owners of the Nanumbas in the area involved in this enquiry.

The second witness for the Nanumba Skin was Alhaji Adam Kanakura Wura who is a Gonja. His evidence in the main supported the boundary as claimed by the Nanumbas and the evidence of the 1st witness for the Nanumbas. The third witness for the Nanumbas was Bukari Mahama, the chief of Sango. He is Dagomba and claimed to be speaking on behalf of Ya-Na i.e the paramount chief of the Dagombas. His evidence also amply supports the claim of the Nanumbas as to their boundary with Dagombas.

The 4th witness was Danasan Monne, a Challa man. From his ecvidence, the stream Kpassa is the boundary between the Nanumbas and the Challas. If his evidence is correct, then he clearly supports the claim of the Nanumbas.

The evidence of this particular witness is of added significance because the Atweodes claim that the Challas are their subjects and from the evidence they are the people living closest to the stream Kpassa on the Atweode side.

The Challas deny being Atweode's but the Atweodes say they are and that a committee is currently hearing a chieftaincy dispute involving the Paramount Stool of the Atweodes and the Challas. The Atweodes alleged that it is this dispute which has made this particular witness to give evidence against the claim of the Atweode Stool.

I shall not comment on the alleged chieftaincy dispute. However, if the evidence of the other witnesses are examined together with this witness's evidence, then the witness in the main agrees with the evidence of the earlier witnesses for Nanumba.

Even if the evidence of this witness is excluded from the evidence there remain the evidence of the 2nd and third witnesses. i.e., the Gonja and Dagomba witnesses supporting the Nanumba claim.

We may now turn to examine the evidence of the Atweode Stool.

The first witness for the Atweode Traditional Area was the Paramount Chief of the Ogulewura of the Atweode Traditional Area.

His evidence on the boundary with the Nanumbas was that he knew the Nanumbas and had a common boundary with them. The boundary begins from the confluence of River Mo and River Oti in the North. It follows River Oti downwards to Suruku, a village which which went under water because of the Akosombo dam. He continued: "the Atweode lands go beyond Suruku further south to the Kapite River or the Otene River. Beyond the Otene River we share boundary with the Nawuri (Easten Gonja). Facing south the Nawuris will be on the west of the Otene River and Atweode lands will be on left hand side i.e., the east of the Otene River. On the south we share boundary with the Adele Traditional Area. This boundary stretches from the confluence of the Oti and Otene Rivers eastwards.

Under cross-examination of by Mr Djabarty, learned counsel for the Nanumbas, he said the River Mo does not form the boundary between the Nanumbas and the Dagombas but rather it was the boundary between the Dagombas and the Atweodes. What this evidence shows is that like the Nanumbas the Atweodes recognises the Gonja and the Dagombas as adjoining boundary owners in the area apart from the Adele Traditional Area with which the witness claimed to share a boundary in the south.

There is therefore, in my opinion, a measure of agreement between the two sides that the Dagombas and the Gonjas are adjoining boundary owners in the area concerned. The evidence of the Atweode Paramount Chief was supported by the evidence of Nana Yaw Blagogee the Adontehene of Atweode Traditional Area, the second witness for the Atweode; Anthony Barkolai Quartey 3rd witness also an Atweode man who is retired education officer and one time District Commissioner for Krachi. The fourth witness for the Atweodes was Kofi Owusu also an Atweode man who claimed to be the Priest of the River Loo or Oti. He also supported the evidence of the Omanhene of the Atweode Traditional Area.

Thus, each of the contesting stools collected 4 witnesses to suppot its claim.

It must be obvious that one significant feature of the list of witnesses is the absence from the list of any witness from the adjoining boundary owners to give evidence in support of the Atweode case. Why did they not call any of the adjoining boundary owners to confirm the boundary as claimed by them?

On the other hand, the Nanumbas did call such witnesses whose evidence did support the claim of that skin. Not only that; the evidence of the Challa man is quite significant. If as it is claimed by the Atweodes the Challas are Atweodes, then the evidence of this witness does not only confirm the Nanumba claim but it seriously destroys the claim of the Atweodes.

It was suggested that the witness was giving evidence against the Atweodes because of a chieftaincy dispute. The substance of the evidence of this witness is that they the Challa live closest to the Kpassa stream, and this stream marks the boundary between their lands and that of the Nannumba. In the absence from the ajoining boundary owners to prove that what this witness told the commission was not the truth. However, they did not do this. In the absence of any evidence to the contrary, I accept the evidence of the witness as true.

On the evidence as a whole, I am satisfied that the Nanumba Skin has clearly established that their version of their eastern boundary ought to be preferred to the boundary as claimed by the Atweode Stool.

However, learned Senior Counsel for the Atweode Stool, who was at one time Attorney-General of this country has argued that, in his words "public policy demand that the Nanumba claim should be rejected". He referred me to various ordinances, Acts and Instruments which shows that the Oti has always been recognized "officially" as the eastern boundary of the Nanumba Skin Lands. I must ask that the argument is quite attractive but in the face of the evidence before me, I can only ask that the facts do not support the view that the Oti is the eastern boundary of the Nanumba Skin Lands.

Apart from the claims and counter claims of the two stools as to various acts of ownership and possession in the area concerned the Nanumba case is amply corroborated by the evidence of the Gonja, Dagomba and Challa witnesses.

Consequently, I reject the claims of the Atweode Stool and uphold the boundary as claimed by the Nanumba Skin.

(SGD.) J. K. ESSIEM
DEPUTY COMMISSIONER.

I have thought it prudent to publish this Kpassa Lands Boundary Sett lement Verdict to educate readers and Ghanaians the rightful owners from Damanko to the Kpassa stream. It has come to the notice of Nanumbas that Konkombas are making false claims of the Kpassa Lands. The rhetorical question I am asking the Konkombas is "the time Nanumbas were in court with Atweodes, where were they to fi le their case and also prove their evidence?" I need an answer from the Konkombas.

It is on record, according to oral literature by the late Bimbilla Lung-Naa Alhaj Abdulai and many other oral literature sources that Konkombas came to Nanung land in 1942 during the reign of Bimbilla Naa Abdulai Kurugu-Kpaa. He was the one who allowed Konkombas to sett le on Nanung land after "The Cow War" at Zegbeli, Dagbon Traditional Area in 1940.

CHAPTER FIVE

DISTORTIONS AND MISCONCEPTIONS OF THE ORAL TRADITION

5.0 INTRODUCTION

The study conducted across the three main Gbewaa Kingdoms in Ghana, revealed some distortions and misconceptions. In this chapter, the writer will attempt to discuss the major distortions and misconceptions to help put the records in order. As information is passed on from one generation to the other, there are very high possibilities of distortions to occur. Unlike Dagbon and Nanung, which have traditional bodies (Tomtom Beaters/Legends) responsible for oral tradition, Mamprugu does not have such a system. As such, distortions, misconceptions, and loss of oral tradition information are very high. It is for these reasons, the writer thought it prudent to develop this chapter for discussion.

5.1 Distortions on the Evolution of the Gbewaa Kingdoms

Many old African writers such as Sekene-mody Cissoko (Histoire de l'afrique Occidentale), Joseph Ki-Zerbo (Histoire de l'afrique Noire) and The History of West Africa are of the view that Tusugu (Tohagu) was the elder, followed by Sitobu and Gmantambu respectively

That the Mamprugu kindom was 45 – 50 years older than Dagbon kindom and Dagbon use to take their skin from the Mamprugu Nayiri.

According to oral tradition, after the power struggled between Zirili and Kufogu in which Zirili killed Kufogu and died shortly led to the death of Naa Gbewaa. Sitobu ascended to the throne. It was during the reign of Naa Sitobu, his son "Nyagsi" sought for fortification to fight, and he went and beheaded the head of Tindana (Female Tindana) at Gambaga where he developed mental illness. After a Dagomba man at Savelugu treated, Nyagsi and they were returning to Yani-Dabari and heard that Naa Sitobu has moved from Yani-Dabari to Bagli. Therefore, they proceeded to Bagli with Nyagsi where Naa Sitobu in the night removed the insignia and kept it on Nyagsi. After this, he cursed sons of Naa Gbewaa not to visit Bagli forever and mysteriously entered the ground. Before he died, he ordered that nobody should inform Tusugu (Tohagu) and Gmantambu what happened that night. The following morning Tusugu (Tohagu) and Gmantambu came to Bagli Tindana's Palace to greet Naa Sitobu only to realized that Nyagsi was sitting in the Chief's insignia. This led to the division of the Gbewaa Kingdom into three main Kingdoms in Northern Ghana at Bagli and Namburugu. Tusugu (Tohagu) became the head as at the time the property, including the insignia was divided into three. The Bagli Tindana called Tusugu (Tohagu) you are now the elder come and take yours. He again called Nyagsi now you represent your father, come, and take yours. Gmantambu was the youngest among the three sons and he was the last person to take his. Bagli Tindana at Namburugu facilitated the sharing process with support from Namburugu Tindana, Salaa Tindana just to mention a few. Hence, this was how Tusugu (Tohagu) became the elder and senior most among the three sons.

The kingdom was one under Naa Gbewaa and Naa Sitobu. The three sons founded their kingdoms at the same time somewhere early 1400. Before they parted at Namburugu, they took an oath of succession and equity that; we are all equal in titles; under no circumstances shall Yaa Naa enskin Nayiri or Bimbilla Naa and the vice versa. To confirm this information, the writer did not only rely on oral tradition from the legends but visited Bagli and Namburugu communities for confirmation of this information by the current Bagli Naa Yakubu Wumbei. *For more information, refer to chapter 2 of this book.* The diagram below is an illustration of the three main Kingdoms of Naa Gbewaa.

NAA GBEWAA (GBEWAA KINGDOM, MID1300)

NAA SITOBU (LATE 1300 – EARLY 1400)

NAA TUSUGU/TOHAGU	NAA NYAGSI (SON OF SITOBU)	NAA GMANTAMBU
(Mamprugu Kingdom, 1400)	(Dagbon Kingdom, 1400)	(Nanung Kingdom, 1400)

There was a succession crisis to the Yani Title after the death of Naa Gungobili. The only alternative was to send the succession issue to Mamprugu for Nayiri to help them resolve it somewhere in the 1700. That was during the reign of Naa Kurugu (Naa Haruna or Naa Bony II) in Mamprugu (*according to the genealogy of Yaa Naas and Mamprugu Nayiris*). Due to the succession and equity oath that their ancestors took at Namburugu/Bagli, Naa Kurugu mediated the case with caution and care. As such, he applied the rule of appellation which Naa Zangina worn. In addition, Naa Kurugu only declared the winner and asked the winner to go back for Yani King Makers to enskin him as Yaa Naa. This is to say; Naa Kurugu of Mamprugu only assisted Dagombas to resolve their succession crisis. Dagbon or Nanung has never taken their skins/titles from Mamprugu.

5.1.1 Kachiogu/Yantaure/Yanenga/Yatura

Some writers and old school of oral tradition are of the view that Kachiogu and Yantaure are two different daughters of Naa Gbewaa, which is not the case. Kachiogu was the name Dagbamba used for the first daughter of Naa Gbewaa. Mossi called her Yanenga, Mamprusi also called Yatura, meaning which part of her you can insult. She was very beautiful. In French, she is called Yantaure. It is the same first daughter of Naa Gbewaa that the various ethnic groups called with different names in their respective languages.

Kachiogu or which of the above was with the father (Naa Gbewaa) for a very long time without getting married. One day, Naa Gbewaa told her to go round the world and make her choice of man she will prefer to marry. Kachiogu or Yantaure could ride a horse very well. Her father allocated a horse to her. When she sat on the horse, the horse took her to far deep in the bush and fortunately, she stopped in front of a group of Mossi men who were on hunting expedition. They asked her where she came from, and she mentioned that she was the daughter of Naa Gbewaa. The leader of the group in the person of Riale proposed love to her, which she accepted. She was with Riale until she delivered a baby boy called Widraugo. Riale parents were afraid of Naa Gbewaa and said they should send a delegation to apologise to Naa Gbewaa. All things been equal, he accepted the apology in good faith and asked them to bring his grandson from the bush for him to see. In Dagbani "Mo ini" means 'bush', so bring the bush child in Dagbani is "Mo ini biya". Hence, the name of Mossi in Dagbani is "Mo i". After the death of Widraugo's grandfather, he started the Mossi kingship. The Mossi therefore are female children of Naa Gbewaa and that is why they are playmates of Dagombas, Mamprusi and Nanumbas because they are cousins.

Kachiogu did not only marry to the Mossi man. She left Riale and came back to the father (Naa Gbewaa) after some time. Whiles she was with the father again, she fell in love with one Dagomba man from Gushegu who was with Naa Gbewaa. They got married and she delivered another baby boy called 'Dang-bora'. Dang-bora was the one who begun Gushegu chieftainship. It is for this reason why the 'Tomtom Beaters' praises' or appellate every Gushegu Chief as "Dang-bora Naa" and the young princes as "Dang-bori Nabia". In addition, it is important to note that, Kachiogu was the princess who set the precedence of every young princess today; to always marry men of their choice and could divorce the man at anytime and marry another man whom she falls in love with. However, this is not to say, they are prostitutes but rather exhibiting the power of princess.

5.1.2 Nanung

According to Cliff S. Maasole, "that one main source of water supply in Bimbilla from time immemorial has been at a spot popularly known as Wan-pu. There is a contention that this place was named after a Konkomba woman who and her husband were the fi rst people ever to sett le there. He further, went on to the etymology as; Pu in the Konkomba language means wife. The names Wanpu, Nyapu, and the like are common with them, and which scarcely exist among the other ethnic communities in the Northern Region". The etymology of the word or name Wan-pu is relative and not only common among the Konkomba language. According to my late Grandmother (Asheitu Alhassan), before Ghana gained independence, the spot was a valley just like the other stretch of the Dam. The only method to fetch water at the valley was by digging holes or mini wells by families or households. Until after Ghana gained independence, this Dam (Wan-pu) was dug. The etymology of the word or name "Wan-pu" in Nanunli or Dagbani is as follows: "Wa" means an expression of surprise and "Puya" which has been shortens as "pu" means a heap, either solid or liquid matter. After they have suffered several years with the holes or mini-wells as source of water, surprisingly saw plenty water as a Dam dug by the Government of Ghana hence, the origin of the name "Wan-pu". Infact the local name is Wan-puni but modern English spelt it Wan-pu.

Cliff S. Maasole claimed that the warrior newcomers, which he referred to Naa Gmantambu and his people, are Nanumbas or aboriginal Dabgamba is more a speculation or lacuna than historical fact. Naa Gmantambu and his people are descendents of Naa Gbewaa from Biun. As such, they were Gurima people who came and conquered the Tindaanba (aboriginal Dagbamba). Naa Gmantambu came to meet the following Tindaanba communities; Daalayili, Sirikpamo now called Bimbilla, Nabang now called Juo, Lanjiri now called Kukuo, Tagnamo or Wumpigu, Varili now called Jilo, Duuni, Ponayili just to mention a few. The simple question is which of these communities is Konkomba origin or common with the Konkomba language? Certainly, none of them. The descendents of Naa Gbewaa did not fight and drive away the indigenous people. Rather, they used their powers to subdue the Tindaanba and inter-marry them as well as adopted the indigenous language. Due to the inter-marriages, the invading families and the original inhabitants have become inter-related.

Naa Gbewaa by origin was not even a Gurima. His ancestors (Tohazie/Tiyawamya) originated from King Shabarko family of ancient Egypt. The Gurima language was equally adopted after his ancestors succeeded the Fetish Priest of Gurima land and took over their kindom.

CHAPTER SIX

ENVIRONMENT AND ECONOMIC ACTIVITIES IN THE GBEWAA KINGDOMS.

6.0 Temperature.

Temperatures are high ranging between 29°C and 41°C. Annual rainfall averages 1268mm with most of it falling within six (6) months i.e., April to September, leaving the rest of the year dry (i.e., when the region comes under the influence of the NE Trades with its associated dry harmattan conditions).

6.1 Vegetation.

The vegetation is the Guinea Savannah type with tall grasses interspersed with drought resistant trees such as Sheanut, dawadawa, acacia, baobab, other drought, and fire-resistant trees are the main tree species found here.

6.2 Soils.

Soils are characteristically heavy and dark-coloured and types available are the Savannah Ochrosols, Savannah Glysols and Ground Water Laterite.

6.3 Economic Trees.

Most of the drought resistant trees are economic trees found in the three main Gbewaa Kingdoms. These include Dawadawa tree (Parkia Filicoides), Baobab tree (Adansonia Digitata), Kapok tree, Mango tree and Sheanut tree (Vitellara paradoxica, formerly Butyrospermum paradoxica).

6.3.1 Dawadawa Tree.

Dawadawa trees grow in the wild. The fruits have enormous economic value. The seed is rich in nutrients such as proteins and it is used in the preparation of soup condiment. The yellow powder that is extracted from the pods equally has protein value and is used in the preparation of very delicious porridge. This yellow powder plays very important role in the economy of the Gbewaa Kingdoms and beyond as it is used as a cooping mechanism in the lean season when there is little, or no food left from the harvest. This period in the annual calendar lies between June – July. However, ownership of dawadawa trees is vested in some subordinate chiefs or titleholders. No individual is entitled to dawadawa fruits. The chief or titleholder may allow an individual farmer on whose farm a number of the dawadawa trees grows to harvest some for his own use. In some communities, they come into terms as to what quantity to be delivered to the titleholder and own the rest. Today this system is failing to work as usual due to the prolonged chieftaincy crisis in some communities in the Gbewaa Kingdoms. The shelled pods are also used to strengthen Swiss buildings and floors.

6.3.2 Baobab Tree.

Baobab seed is used for the preparation of soup condiment similar to that of dawadawa. The taste of the two, however, differs. The leaves of the Boabab is used vegetable for the preparation of soup. The leaves sre dried for preervation. The white powder extracted from the pod of the baobab fruit is also edible and used to prepare local drinks. The shelled pods are burned into soda-ash, which is used in the preparation of soap. Baobab trees also have spiritual values.

6.3.3 Kapok Tree.

The seed from Kapok tree is richer in proteins and oil. It is also used in the preparation of soup condiment similar to that of baobab. The floss of Kapok is used for stuffing cushions, pillows, and mattresses. This gives the tree its commercial value. The shells of kapok may be burnt, and the ash used in the preparation of soap.

6.3.4 Mango.

Mango trees are planted around compounds at individual homes for fruits, shade and serve as wind brakes. Some farmers cultivate the local mango on small-scale plantations for income. Today mango production has gained international recognition with the introduction of improved varieties of grafted mango such as Kieth and Kent, which are accepted and highly demanded by the international markets. A good number of hectares of land have been used for the cultivation of these improved varieties for export.

6.3.5 Nim Tree.

Nim tree is a foreign tree species in the Gbewaa Kingdoms. However, it is gradually gaining importance as an economic tree. The activities of man such as farming and urbanization are depleting wood, which are used as rafters. Wood from the nim tree, though not as hard as local species used for rafters, is now becoming the best substitute. The leaves also have medicinal purposes as it is boiled and used for the treatment of fever or malaria. Just like the mango tree, nim trees are also planted round or infront of houses to provide shade for resting after the day's labour or non-farming days e.g., Fridays. Young nim plants or the twigs of nim often provide chewing sticks for some people in the society.

6.3.6 Shea Tree.

Shea trees are most important economic trees with high industrial value that also grows in the wild. It variously reported that European explorers first recorded Shea in the early 18th century and by the 1920s. The start point of Shea butter is the Sheanut tree, (*Vitellara paradoxica*, formerly *Butyrospermum paradoxica*), a semi-deciduous tree that survives ravaging annual bush fires characteristic of the Sahel savannah grasslands where it abounds.

Shea nut trees grow semi-wild, and women have harvested them for decades, pounding them into butter and oil to use in cooking or as a moisturizing cream. About 4-5 million women in West Africa are involved in the collection, processing, and marketing of Shea nuts and butter, providing about 80 percent of their incomes.

The trees are truly multi-purpose and are highly valued not only for the economic and dietary value of the cooking oil, but also for the fruit pulp, bark, roots, and leaves, which are used in traditional medicines and for the wood and charcoal, used for building and cooking fuel.

Many vernacular names are used for Vitellaria, which reflects its extensive range of occurrence – nearly 5,000km from Senegal (West Africa) to Uganda (East Africa) across the African Continent. It usually grows to an average height of about 15m with profuse branches and a thick waxy and deeply fissured bark that makes it fire resistant. The Shea tree grows naturally in the wild in the dry Savannah belt of West Africa from Senegal in the west to Sudan in the east, and onto the foothills of the Ethiopian highlands. It occurs in 19 countries across the African continent, namely Benin, Ghana, Chad, Burkina Faso, Cameroon, Central African Republic, Ethiopia, Guinea Bissau, Cote D'Ivoire, Mali, Niger, Nigeria, Senegal, Sierra Leone, Sudan, Togo, Uganda, Zaire, and Guinea. Mali is the largest producer.

In Ghana (FAO, 1988a), *V. paradoxica* occurs extensively in the Sudan Savannah and less abundantly in the Guinea Savannah. The Shea tree occurs over almost the entire area of Northern Ghana, over about 77,670 square kilometers in Western Dagomba, Southern Mamprusi, Western Gonja, Lawra, Tumu, Wa and Nanumba with Eastern Gonja having the densest stands. There is sparse Shea tree cover found in Brong-Ahafo, Ashanti, and the Eastern and Volta regions in the south of Ghana.

Considerable volumes of literature exist on the ecology of the Shea tree including its yield. According to these authors, the trees are ravaged by annual bushfires that usually burn the undergrowth and cause stunted growth of the trees in the wild. Under these conditions, the trees attain heights of only 6.1 meters and girths of about 61cm. However, under protected conditions (e.g., on cultivated lands and on the fringes of settlements) the trees can reach heights of about 15 meters and girths of 175cm. The trees grow slowly from seeds, taking about 30 years to reach maturity, but limiting or stressful conditions such as bushfires and harsh weather can reduce this. The Shea tree has no capacity for vegetative regeneration and can only be propagated by seed.

Boffa, (1999) for instance asserts that the Shea belt comprises more than 500 million fruiting trees and FAO, estimate total African production at approximately 1,760,000 metric tons of Shea nuts. However, due to the scattered nature of the crop over an extensive and remote landscape, it is estimated that only a third of this amount is collected. This is a huge production given that there are no Shea plantations and farmers only start to protect trees once they are more than saplings as part of traditional parkland farming system. However, most of the nuts are not harvested and hence the value of the market is considerably less than its potential. Of the 35% of potential nuts gathered, local butter processing takes the bulk of this at 85% from which an estimated 100,000 Metric tons of local butter is produced.

Studies by Ruyssen 1957, found that productivity in subspecies *V. paradoxa* rises rapidly in the age range 40-50 years and stabilises in trees of 100-200 years before declining in aging plants of 200-400 years. Due to the adverse weather conditions in the Sahel, fruit production fluctuates considerably from tree to tree and between seasons. An average fruit yield per tree was conservatively estimated at 15-20 kg / year.[1]

Despite interest by Governments and FAO expert panels to develop Shea industries, little successful attempts have been made to domesticate the crop and essentially. Therefore, Shea remains a wild fruit that is seasonally gathered by the local community.[2]

6.3.6 .1 Shea Butter Potentials.

Traditional Shea butter extraction is a major income-generating activity for women in the Northern and Upper regions of Ghana. Since 1998 over 32,000 metric tons of Shea nuts have been exported from Ghana annually, generating about US$7,000,000 revenue per year. Available figures demonstrate that Ghana is certainly the biggest exporter of home-produced Shea related products in the ECOWAS sub-region. Since 1997, the Ghana Export Promotion Council has monitored annual exports of Shea butter ranging between 32,000 and 45,000 ton of dry Shea kernel mainly traded by Kassardjan and Olam for processing by Aarhus United in Denmark, Karlsham in Sweden, Loders Crocklaan in Holland, or Fuji Oils in Japan. This period has also shown an exponential increase in Shea butter exports from virtually zero in the early nineties to over 2,500 Metric tons by the end of 2002. Much of this increase in production can be linked to in-country mechanical processing for refining abroad, although women's groups are also known to process a significant proportion.

For industrial processors, Shea is a low-cost substitute product sold mainly into the cocoa butter equivalent markets and the bulk of Shea produced in West Africa supplies this market. However, there has been a renewed interest from the high value cosmetics companies and for this market sector, the very fact that Shea remains a wilderness crop, which is collected and processed by women's groups in remote rural areas, creates a fashionable marketing scenario. Further, recent changes in European Union regulations on the use of substitutes for cocoa butter have increased demand for Shea butter from chocolate confectioners, as it is now possible to blend up to 5% non cocoa butter equivalents into chocolate products. This development provides an excellent opportunity to expand Shea production as there will continue to be a high demand for Shea butter in the international market particularly from the chocolate industry. Further, some economic recovery in the former Soviet Kingdoms has led to increased demand for Shea for input into their confectionary products. There is also a renewed interest in Shea butter from the cosmetics industry.

Depending on the process and kernel quality, wide ranges of yields from traditional extraction methods have been reported, with the highest extraction rates of 83 % (of available fat) obtained by Dagomba women near Tamale. Many attempts have been made to introduce semi-industrial methods for Shea butter extraction (roasters, kneaders, efficient stoves, etc), because of the supposedly low yielding and resource intensive traditional processes. Unfortunately, due to poor technology, unreliable harvests, poor communication, and high start-up costs, many of these projects have not been successful. The most commonly utilized 'improved' technology is the plate-grinder, powered by either electricity or diesel engines, now seen throughout Northern Ghana, and used for grinding every agricultural product imaginable.

Shea butter is hard at room temperature due to the composition of oils within the nuts, which have a high stearin: olein ratio. Stearin is a solid fat fraction and Olien is an oil-like liquid at room temperature, fractions, the oil, and the fat are used as raw materials in cooking oil, margarine, cosmetics, soap, detergents and candles.

6.3.6.2 Alternative Applications & Uses of Shea Butter.

Shea butter is the main edible oil for the people of northern Ghana, being the most important source of fatty acids and glycerol in their diet. It is an unguent for the skin. It also has anti-microbial properties, which gives it a place in herbal medicine. It is also used in the pharmaceutical and cosmetic industries as an important raw material and/or a precursor for the manufacture of soaps, candles, and cosmetics. Shea butter is used as a sedative or anodyne for the treatment of sprains, dislocations and the relief of minor aches and pains. Other important uses include its use as an anti-microbial agent for promotion of rapid healing of wounds, as a pan-releasing agent in bread baking and as a lubricant for donkey carts. Its by-products, the brown solid that is left after extracting the oil and the hard protective shell, are used as a waterproofing material on the walls of mud-buildings to protect them from the eroding forces of the wind and rain. Poor quality butter is not only applied to earthen walls but also to doors, windows, and even beehives as a waterproofing agent. In a traditional setting, Shea butter of poor quality is used as an illuminant (or fuel, in lamps or as candles).

As a cosmetic, it is used as a moisturizer, for dressing hair and for protection against the weather and sun. It is used as a rub to relieve rheumatic and joint pains and is applied to activate healing in wounds and in cases of dislocation, swelling and bruising. It is widely used to treat skin problems such as dryness, sunburn, burns, ulcers, and dermatitis and to massage pregnant women and small children.

Having a high melting point of between (32-45°C) and being close to body temperature are attributes that make it particularly suitable as a base for ointments and medicines. It is also used to treat horses internally and externally for girth galls and other sores. The healing properties of Shea butter are believed to be partly attributable to the presence of allantoin, a substance known to stimulate the growth of healthy tissue in ulcerous wounds. It is used as "white oil" to anoint the dead in Niger and is placed in traditional ritual shrines.

Refuse-water from production of Shea butter is used as termite repellent and wall paint against rain erosion of walls. In Burkina Faso, Shea butter is used to protect against insect damage to cowpeas. Research has shown that after treatment with Shea butter a reduction occurs in the life span and fertility of the insects and hence the infestation rate. Shea butter, however, is not as effective as cottonseed or groundnut oil.

6.3.6.3 Flowers, Fruit and Nuts.

The Shea nut serves as the main source of livelihood for the rural women and children who are engaged in its gathering. Some ethnic groups make the flowers into edible fritters. The fruit pulp, being a valuable food source, is also taken for its slightly laxative properties. Although not widespread, Shea nut cake is used for cattle feed, and eaten raw by children. The residual meal, as in the case with Shea butter, is also used as a waterproofing agent to repair and mend cracks in the exterior walls of mud huts, windows, doors, and traditional beehives. The sticky black residue, which remains after the clarification of the butter, is used for filling cracks in hut walls and as a substitute for kerosene when lighting firewood. The husks reportedly make a good mulch and fertilizer and are also used as fuel on three stone fires.

6.3.6.4 Industrial Uses.

Research into the properties and potential industrial uses of Shea butter began in the first few decades of the last century. Previously, it was used in edible fats and margarine, e.g., Oleine, and was only beginning to attract the soap and perfume industry when interest ceased because of the 2nd World War. Revival of the Shea industry after the war suffered serious setbacks from an insufficient pricing mechanism, logistical problems of transport (low availability and unpredictable) unable to cope with the supply of the nuts, thus making the ventures economically non-viable. During the mid 1960s, Shea trade re-emerged when Japanese traders joined their European counterparts, which saw a considerable expansion of the industry, particularly in the cosmetics and confectionery industry barely a decade thereafter.

Shea butter has several industrial applications, but the majority of kernels (approximately 95%) provides an important raw material for Cocoa Butter Replacers (CBRs) and is used for manufacturing chocolate and other confectionery. Minor uses include cosmetics and pharmaceuticals. In Ghana, the export market for CBRs is shared by Unilever (UK), Arhus (Denmark), Fuji Itoh and Kaneka-Mitsubishi (Japan) and Karlsham (Sweden).

6.4 Agriculture.

The Gbewaa Kingdoms are largely agricultural with about 80% of the population depends on agriculture. Crops that are cultivated include the following: Yam, Cassava, Rice, Maize, Guinea corn/Sorghum, Soybeans, Millet, Groundnuts, and some vegetables. They also rear animals such as Cattle, Sheep, Goat, Poultry and Pigs.

Most of the farmers are smallholder or peasant farmers. Modern Dagbon is noted for major producers of rice, groundnut, and maize. Naumba area is noted as major producers of yam and cassava.

CHAPTER SEVEN

7.0 SLAVE TRADE AND ITS RESISTANCE IN THE GBEWAA KINGDOMS.

7.1 Transatlantic Slave Trade.

Cape Coast which is located on the shore of the Atlantic Ocean and the Cape Coast Castle was one of the last points of contact for the enslaved Africans before they were taken away from the continent to work on the plantations of the New World[6].

When it comes to making slave-trade heritage, Northern Ghana towns such as, Paga have a lot to offer. Beyond the subliminal spiritual significance of the pilgrimage lies the economic potential. Northern Ghana's linkage with the Transatlantic slave trade is too strong to be taken lightly. From Sandema to Yendi, Gwollu to Nalerigu the landscape is replete with relics. (Akpabli 2001).

Figure 1Salaga Slave Wells & Bath where Slaves were Bathed.

What is striking in this statement is the fact that all the sites that are mentioned, including the Pikworo Slave Camp at Paga, Saakpuli Slave Market, Salaga Slave Market, Salaga Slave Wells & Bath, Juole Defense-Wall are primarily connected to the slave raids of the Zabarima traders, Babatu and Samori in the late nineteenth century. By that time, the transatlantic slave trade had already been abolished for a few decades; the British slave trade activity officially ceased in 1807, France followed in 1848, and Brazil, which was reluctant to abolish the lucrative business, was forced to do so in 1852. Even though the official abolition did not lead to a complete halt in slaving activities but rather in an increase in illegal slave exports in some areas, the eventual ending of the institution of slavery in the Americas also marked the end of the transatlantic slave trade[11]. In the British colonies, this was done in 1834, in the United States in 1865 and finally in Brazil in 1888. By then the industrial revolution had changed the face of Euro-American economy and the major European powers began their scramble for Africa in order to facilitate direct colonial exploitation. However, the inner-African and indigenous slave trade went on for a longer period. In Asante and the Northern territories of the Gold Coast, laws on the emancipation of slaves were passed as late as 1908, institution of slavery still operating illegally at least up to 1928 (cf Perbi 2002: 193 – 205).

Figure 2: Salaga Slave Market - Captured Slaves were Chained onto this Baobab Tree.

Although the slave sites in Northern Ghana are primarily related to the slave raids of the late nineteenth century, the earlier transatlantic slave trade had made impact here, too. Mossi and Hausa traders operated in those areas long before Babatu and Samori entered the historical stage (cf Der 1998).

7.2 Resistance of Slave Trade in Northern Ghana by Traditional Rulers.

Before the passage of law in 1908, traditional rulers in the Gbewaa Kingdoms resisted slave activities by Babatu and Samori among others by fighting them. This led to a war between Dagombas and Zabarima people in the present-day Niger. The war was resolved by the signing of peace treaty between Dagombas and Zabarimas. This paved a way for the Babatu and Samori continue their slave trade in the Non-Gbewaa Kingdoms. In the light of this, Bolga and Bongo joined the Gbewaa Kingdoms to be freed from Babatu and Samori slave activities. The Builsa people finally defeated Babatu and Samori in a war between the Builsa and the Slave Traders (Babatu and Samori). They took their weapons and dumped them under a Tree. The spot has become a shrine in the Builsa land and annual rituals are performed there to mark their success over the Zabarima slave raiders. Babatu did not returned to his home country but rather went and settled in Yendi and that was where he retired from slave trade. The grave of Babatu can still be found in Yendi with the slave chains and shackles.

Figure 3: Babatu Grave at Yendi

The construction of slave defense walls at Gwollu, Nalerigu (built with milk & human parts) and Juole were part of the efforts explored by traditional rulers to resist the activities of slave trade in Northern Ghana.

Figure 4: Defense Wall at Gwollu

Figure 5: Defense Wall at Nalerigu

7.3 Conclusion.

Africans were themselves capturing their fellow Africans as slaves to the Whiteman and seen as a lucrative business without considering the negative impact.

Africans in the diaspora can be traced to the United State of America and Europe. The question I could not find answer to, is Africans who were enslaved and exported to the Arabian. Where are they today or where can we find them?

There was intra African slave trade or indigenous slave trade. Since the laws on the emancipation of slaves were passed as late as 1908. By 1930s slaves were integrated in the society. Today in Northern Ghana, one cannot trace who was a slave in this modern society.

Slave trade had been abolished and Africa has gained independence from our colonial masters. The rhetorical question, is Africa totally free from the Whiteman? The answer is no, because Africa gained only physical independence and psychologically African leaders have been remoted by the white man. Until we emancipate ourselves from mental slavery before we can gain psychological independence from the Whiteman.

Psychological independence is the key to Africa socio-economic development. Africa has a population of 1.2 billion which is very good for market attraction. The sad news is that Africa is performing less than 17% for trade among Africans (Ghana National Export Development Strategy, 2020).

African leaders have initiated African Continental Free Trade Area (AFCFTA). 54 out 55 countries have signed except Eritrea. This initiative is to boost trade among Africans. The head office is located in Accra, Ghana. AFCFTA is scheduled to start in 2021.

The number of slave sites in Northern Ghana is a clear justification that most African Diasporas came from Northern Ghana and not the Southern Part of Ghana. Cape Coast which is located on the shore of the Atlantic Ocean and the Cape Coast Castle was one of the last points of contact for the enslaved Africans and not their origins.

APPENDIX I:

GENEALOGY OF YANI CHIEFS' (YAA NANIMA)

Naa Nyagsi, son of Sitobu
Naa Zulande, son of Nyagsi
Naa Nagalogu, son of Zulande
Naa Dalugudamda (Datorili), son of Nyagsi
Naa Briguyomda, son of Nyagsi
Naa Zoligu, son of Dalugudamda
Naa Zongman (Zuu Zong), son of Zoligu
Naa Ninmitooni, son of Zoligu
Naa Dimani, son of Zoligu
Naa Yanzoo, son Zoligu
Naa Dariziegu, son of Zongman
Naa Luro, son of Zoligu
Naa Tituguri, son of Luro
Naa Zagale, son of Luro
Naa Zokuli (Dawuni), son of Luro
Naa Gungobili (Wumbei), son of Luro
Naa Zangina, son of Tituguri 1700 – 1718
Naa Andani Sigli, son of Zagale 1718 – 1738
Naa Binbiegu (Zuu Jingli or Ziblim), son of Zangina 1738 – 1740
Naa Gariba, son of Zangina 1740 – 1745
Naa Saa-Lana Ziblim, son of Andani Sigli 1745 – 1763
Naa Ziblim Bandamda, son of Gariba
Naa Andani Jangbariga, son of Gariba
Naa Mahami, son of Ziblim Bandamda
Naa Ziblim Kulunku, son of Andani Jangbariga
Naa Sumani Zoli, son of Mahami
Naa Yakubu I, son of Andani Jangbariga 1824 – 1849

Naa Abudulai I, son of Yakubu I 1849 – 1876
Naa Andani II, son of Yakubu I 1876 – 1899
Naa Alhassan, son of Abudulai I 1900 – 1917
Naa Abudulai II (Abudu), son of Alhassan 1920 – 1938
Naa Mahama II, son of Andani II 1938 – 1948
Naa Mahama III, son of Alhassan 1948 – 1953
Naa Abuduai III, son of Mahama III 1954 – 1967
Naa Andani III, son of Mahama II 1968 – 1969
Naa Mahadu Abudulai IV, son of Abudulai III 1969 – 1974
Naa Yakubu Andani II, son of Andani III 1974 – 2002
Naa Abubakari Mahama II, son of Naa Mahama II 18th January 2019 ……..

APPENDIX II:

GENEALOGY OF MAMPRUGU CHIEFS' (NAYIRIS)

Naa Tohagu (Tusugu), son of Naa Gbewaa 1400 -1421
Naa Kotam (Bang-marigu) 1421 – 1461
Naa Gbingima (Kamsulgu Lasure) 1461 – 1464
Naa Zomsaa (Kumasure Kasuri) 1464 -1491
Naa Moari (Mahami I/Namwali) 1494 – 1499
Naa Tampuri (Tampuri) 1499 – 1529
Naa Sigri (Ziblim Bantaga)
Naa ŋ◉ntonaa (Nantuwa)
Naa Tabiya (Zontuwa Sulemana)
Naa Jirnga (Yamusah I)
Naa Kurugu (Haruna/Naa Bonyii) 1697 -1712
Naa Piisim (Andani/Issakazia) 1712 – 1737
Naa Benaa (Mahami II) 1737 -1742
Naa Zia (Salifu Mahami I) 1742 – 1743
Naa Kuligu Baa (Mahami III) 1743 – 1773
Naa Satang-Kugri (Salifu Mahami II) 1773 – 1806
Naa Dam-Bongu (Dahamani Mahami) 1806 – 1809
Naa Nyongu (Dawuda Salifu) 1809 – 1839
Naa Pa'ari (Azabu Salifu) 1839 – 1864
Naa Bariga II (Yamusah Salifu II) 1864 - 1901
Naa Sigri (Sulemana Azabu I) 1901 – 1905
Naa Zori (Zing-nya Salifu) 1906 – 1909
Naa Wugba (Mahami Dawuda IV) 1909 – 1915
Naa Waafu (Mahami Yamusah V) 1915 – 1933
Naa Zulim (Badimsugru Azabu) 1933 – 1943
Naa Salima (Salifu Zing-nya III) 1943 – 1943
Naa Soro (Abudulai Sulemana I) 1943 – 1947

Naa Sheriga (Abudulai Mahami II) 1947 – 1966
Naa Bongu (Adam Badimsugru) 1967 – 1985
Naa Saa (Sulemana Salifu II) 1986 – 1987
Naa Gamni (Abdulai Mahamadu III) 1987 – 2003
Naa Bohagu II (Mahami Abdulai) 26th January 2004 ………

APPENDIX III:

GENEALOGY OF NANUNG/ BIMBILLA CHIEFS'

Naa Gmantambu, son of Naa Gbewaa
Naa Sulgme
Naa Kumkayo ri, son of Gmantambu
Naa Dogiporigu, son of Sulgme
Naa Badariga
Naa Na i Baarigu
Naa Saa
Naa Koŋa
Naa Kunbalinkulga
Naa Nyelinbolgu, son of Kunbalinkulga
Naa Wobgu (Naa Pampamli or Mahamuda)
Naa Saa-kpang (Naa Damba)
Naa Sulgu (Naa Maamani), son of Wobgu/Mahamuda
Naa Gbuguma (Naa Azuma)
Naa Nyong (Naa Imoro), son of Naa Damba
Naa Bulali-bila (Naa Kurugu-kpaa) son of Nakpa-Naa Sanboni
Naa Abarika I, (Naa Bang) son of Dakpam-Naa Kpanjogu
Naa Shero, son of Naa Gbuguma
Naa Natogmah I (Naa Peinkpaa), son of Naa Abarika I
Naa Kalo (Naa Mahama), son of Naa Gbuguma
Naa Toli (Naa Dahamani) son of Naa Abarika I
Naa Yakubu Savigu
Naa Wahu (Naa Abalsi)
Naa Ziblim Kuntibsa son of Nakpaa Naa Andani
Naa Mahami
Naa Haruna son of Gundow Naa Gnunbaakum
Naa Salifu, son of Naa Peinkpaa

Naa Abdulai Kurugu-kpaa 1926 – 1944
Naa Natogmah II, son of Dakpam-Naa Attah 1944 – 1959
Naa Dassana, son of Naa Abdulai 1959 – 1981
Naa Abarika Attah II, son of Dakpam-Naa Attah 1983 – 1999

BIBLIOGRAPHY

Accra Declaration. 1995 on the WTO-UNESCO Cultural Tourism Programme "The Slave Route, 4th April 1995, Accra, Ghana, Adopted on 29th April 1995, in Durban, South Africa, by the 27th meeting of the Regional Commission for Africa of the World Tourism Organization, Paris, UNESCO.

Akpabli, K. 2001. A Pilgrimage to Paga; The Tourist November 2001: N.P.

Cliff S. Maasole - The Konkomba and Their Neighbours, 2006

Costheta Consults Gh. Ltd, 2009 (Feasibility Report on Shea Nuts Processing)

Der, B. G. 1998. The Slave Trade in Northern Ghana. Accra: Woeli.

Featured Article by Fusheini Yakubu, Slave Trade and Its Resistance in the Gbewaa States, 27th November 2020.

Ghana National Export Development Strategy, 2020.

Ibrahim Mahama - History and Tradition of Dagbon, 2004.

Intercontinental Shea Nuts Project, 2009 (Feasibility Report on Shea Nuts Processing).

Illiasu A.A. 1970, 'Asante's relations with Dagomba, C.1740 -1884', The Ghana Social Science Juornal I (2)

In the Stool Lands Boundaris Settlement Commission Sitting at the Meeting Room 4, State House Accra Tuesday, 25th Day of September 1979, Before MR J. K. Essiem, Deputy Commissioner between Nanumba and Shiare.

Joseph Ki-Zerbo - Histoire de l'afrique Noire

Millennium Youth Skills and Development Centre (MILLYSDEC), 2009 (Feasibility Report on Shea Nuts Processing)

Manoukian, Madeline, 1952, Tribes of the Northern Territories of the Gold Coast (Ethnographic Survey of Africa. West Africa pt V), London International African Institute.

Osei Kwadwo - An Outline of Asante History, Part 1- Third Edition, 2004.

Rattray, R. S. 1932. The Tribes of the Ashanti Hinterland, 2 vols. (Oxfford: Clarend on Press' repr. 1969).

Report by His Majesty's Government in the United Kingdom of Great Britain and Northern Ireland to the Council of the League of Nations on the Administration of Togoland under British Mandate for the year 1930

Reports by His Majesty's Government to the Council of the League of Nations on the Administration of Togoland under British Mandate for the years; 1931, 1933, 1935 and 1949.

Sekene-mody Cissoko - Histoire de l'afrique Occidentale, 1850.

Shinnie, P. and P. Ozanne. 1972 Excavation at Yani Dabari' Transactions of the Historical Society of Ghana No. 6.

Sibidow, S. M. 1969 Background of the Yendi Skin Crisis (Accra, Yenzow)

Tamakloe, E. F. 1931 A Brief History of the Dagbamba People (Accra, Government Printer).

Topics in West African History, New Edition by Adu Boahen with J.F. Ade Ajayi and Michael Tidy - 1992

www.ingramcontent.com/pod-product-compliance
Lightning Source LLC
Chambersburg PA
CBHW060246030426
42335CB00014B/1617